BABYCARE
DAY BY DAY

Dr Frances Williams

CARROLL & BROWN

This edition first published in 2013 in the
United States by

Carroll & Brown
20 Lonsdale Road London NW6 6RD

Copyright © Carroll & Brown Limited 2012

Library of Congress Cataloging-in-Publication Data

Williams, Frances, Dr.

Babycare day by day / Frances Williams. -- U.S. ed.

p. cm.

Includes index.

ISBN 978-1-909066-06-9 (hardback spiral : alk. paper)

1. Newborn infants--Care. 2. Newborn infants--Health and hygiene.
3. Child care. I. Title.

RJ253.W544 2013

618.92'01--dc23

2012029367

ISBN 978-1-909066-06-9

10 9 8 7 6 5 4 3 2 1

Printed in China

Note: No information provided in this book should be
construed as a personal diagnosis or treatment. Always
consult with your own physician(s) as regards your own care.

Suppliers
Thanks to Mothercare, for equipment shown p32 (bottom left), p50 and p90.
Thanks to BabyBjörn, for equipment shown p87 (top right).

Photolibrary.com
p4 (bottom right), p16, p28, p30 and p37.

CONTENTS

FOREWORD

Taking care of a baby is round-the-clock work and a hands-on occupation, and once a baby arrives, all parents suddenly realize exactly what it means to "have their hands full!" Having been carried around for the first nine months of their lives, babies yearn to be in constant contact with their caregivers. Rare is the parent who very shortly doesn't wish he or she had an extra pair of hands when it comes to taking care of a baby, particularly at such nerve-racking times as getting a baby bathed and dressed.

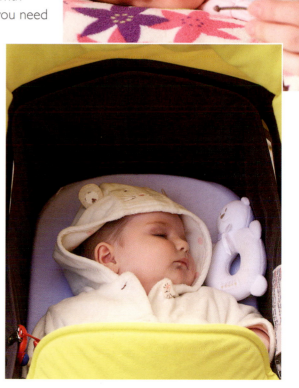

Now help is at hand for new parents and others unfamiliar with basic babycare. In *Babycare Day by Day,* you'll find everything you need to know in order to hold, feed, carry, change, dress, bath, soothe, play with, massage, and comfort your newborn baby up to his or her first birthday. There is also much useful information on developmental milestones, taking care of an ill baby, and essential first aid. Best of all, the book can be stood up next to where you are caring for your baby so you can access all the information while keeping your hands on your baby when needed. And when you do have more time, there is a great deal of useful information to read and consider on the top pages.

Step-by-step photographs illustrate all the stages of essential care routines such as changing a diaper, putting on a onesie, using a baby carrier, or preparing a bottle. Short, concise captions make following the steps easy.

Parenting skills are not inborn, they have to be acquired. I hope this book helps new parents, grandparents, babysitters, and child carers gain the confidence and competence necessary not only to care for their babies but to enjoy doing so.

HANDLING YOUR BABY

You will be picking up and carrying your baby a great deal during the first few months and this should always be done gently and smoothly so as not to frighten him. Though a baby is usually more robust than you might think, it's important never to handle your baby roughly or shake him. When picking up your baby always hold him close, support his head, and make reassuring sounds.

PICKING UP FROM A FACE-UP POSITION

Your young baby should always be put on his back to sleep and, obviously, he will be on his back for diaper changing, so you will most often pick him up from a supine, or face-up, position.

If your baby is sleeping, it is a good idea to rouse him gently before lifting, as until you become practiced at lifting, your baby may find the motion rather startling, which can cause him to cry. Talking to your baby softly or gently stroking his cheek as you prepare to pick him up will help to reassure him.

To make it easy on your back, always bend down close to your baby before lifting him up.

A safe haven
Held cradled in your arms, your baby feels secure at your nearness. Being held in a position where he can feel your pulse or hear your heartbeat is comforting.

PICKING UP FROM A FACE-UP POSITION

1 **Support your baby's neck and bottom as you lift** Lean in close to your baby and slide one hand under his head and neck and the other beneath his bottom. Take his weight in your hands and begin to lift. If he's awake, a few calm words from you will reassure him and give him a sense of security.

2 **Gently raise him higher** Still leaning well forward and making sure his head is well supported, raise your baby smoothly from the surface. Try to keep his head slightly above the level of the rest of his body. If he's awake, talk to him and establish eye contact as you lift.

3 **Rest him in the crook of your elbow** As you bring your baby close to your chest, slide the hand supporting his bottom up to support his back. Bend and extend your other arm so that it lies along his body and his head is supported in the crook of your elbow.

Laying your baby down

Simply perform steps 1 and 2 in reverse: ease your baby gently away from your body, while supporting his head and neck with one hand and his bottom with the other.

PICKING UP FROM A FACE-DOWN POSITION

Most of the time you will be picking up a young baby from a supine, or face-up, position, as this is the safest position for a baby to lie in. However, there will be occasions when you have to pick your baby up from a face-down, or prone, position, for instance, when she is put on her tummy to play or when she rolls over during sleep (which is likely to happen more and more often as she gets older).

Initially, you may find this maneuver awkward, but with experience, it will soon feel natural. The guidelines provided should give you confidence.

As with all lifting, take care to make it easy on your back. Changing tables, crib mattresses and baby baths should all be at about waist level, which will make your movements both safer and more comfortable. Bend your knees, not your back.

Your older baby

By about six months of age, your baby should become quite adept at rolling from her back on to her front. So, even if you lay her down on her back, she may turn over and you will have to pick her up from a face-down, or prone, position.

Tummy time
For her proper development, even when very young, your baby should spend some time on her front, but don't leave her alone in this position.

PICKING UP FROM A FACE-DOWN POSITION

1 **Support your baby's tummy and head** Slide one hand between your baby's legs so that your palm rests on her abdomen and chest. Gently position your other hand under her cheek so she faces one side and her head is well supported and in line with the rest of her body.

2 **Slowly raise your baby up**, making sure her body weight is well supported by sliding the hand that was under her cheek around to her chest and maintaining your hold of her lower body. As you lift her up, gently start to rotate her toward you. Keep your baby's head raised slightly above the rest of her body.

3 **Cradle her in your arms** As you turn your baby toward you, slide the hand you had between her legs underneath her bottom. Lower your other arm so your baby's head rests in the crook of your elbow, and your forearm supports her along her length. Hold her close.

HOLDING YOUR BABY

All babies enjoy physical contact; in fact, they need to be held and cuddled to feel secure and loved. As a new parent you will find yourself holding your baby for a great deal of his waking hours. It is important, however, never to do anything that could put your baby in danger while you hold him—like picking up a pan of hot water or stretching to reach something.

Your newborn will want to be held close to you. He has only recently emerged from the confined space of your uterus so he will feel happier and more comfortable if he is gently, but securely, held in your arms with his limbs close to his body.

For your part, holding your baby will give you the opportunity to watch as his expressions change, and he discovers more about the world around him.

Until your baby can hold his head up by himself, you will need to be careful to support his neck whenever you lift or hold him.

Your older baby

Once your baby has gained sufficient control over his neck and can assume an upright head posture, at around four months, he will need less support. There are a number of ways to carry your baby to give him a different view of his surroundings.

Front facing forward
Hold your baby with his back against you, with one arm under his arm and across his chest. Use your other hand to support his bottom.

On your hip
Sit your baby astride your hip with his legs either side of your body and support him with one hand across his back. If his legs don't grip well enough, use your other hand as extra support for his bottom.

HOLDING YOUR YOUNG BABY

Face down in your arms
Support your baby's head in the crook of your elbow with your forearm supporting his chest. Put your other arm between his legs so that your hand rests on his tummy.

Face up in your arms
Support your baby's back in the crook of one elbow with your other arm under his bottom. You can hold him with just one arm, but make sure it cradles his head, back, and bottom. Holding your baby with two hands, however, offers greater support.

Nestled against your shoulder
Use one hand to support your baby's bottom and the other to protect his neck and upper back.

USING A SLING

Essentially a length of fabric, a sling will hold your baby close to your chest, while she is being carried indoors and out. Some styles leave the legs and arms free; others cover the whole baby. They tend not to offer a baby as much support as carriers (see page 14), so many models are more suitable for younger babies—but always check the manufacturer's guidelines and fitting instructions carefully.

A sling or wrap (which generally contains more fabric than a simple sling) enables you to go about your daily tasks while keeping your baby snug and secure. Your baby will enjoy this feeling of closeness. In fact, the majority of parents say that they feel much closer to their babies when they practice "baby wearing." If you and your partner are both going to use the sling or wrap, check that it is adjustable for your different sizes.

Slings enable you to hold your baby in a variety of positions—from almost flat to upright. Your baby can face toward you, upward, or outward. As the fabric could block your baby's nose and mouth, you must never put your baby face downward in a sling nor hold her in one so that her chin curves down to her chest, which also restricts breathing.

When you're calculating how many layers of clothing your baby needs (see page 50), bear in mind that a sling or wrap counts as one layer, and that it can get quite warm inside the pouch. Check regularly that she is not too hot by feeling the side of her neck—it should not feel at all sweaty.

Constant company
A sling or wrap keeps a tiny baby close to you, where she is happiest and reassured by hearing your voice and heartbeat and feeling your movement as you go about your daily routine.

GETTING YOUR BABY INTO A SLING

1 **Put on the sling** Follow the manufacturer's instructions, so the ends go around your waist and over opposite shoulders and the label is centered.

2 **Tie off at the back of your waist** underneath the "X" formed by the fabric.

3 **Place your baby inside** Gently lift your baby into the pouch formed by the "X" across your chest—the smaller the baby, the higher the "X" should be.

4 **Adjust the pouch** Make sure your baby is secure before you raise the pouch fabric up her back. A tiny baby's legs will tuck in the pouch; an older baby's will hang free.

TAKE CARE

If your baby was premature or suffers from breathing problems or has a cold, seek advice before using a sling.

A sling should fit snugly against your body so that your baby is kept tight against your chest, rather than on your waist or hips.

Your baby's face and chest should always face upward with her body and chin off her chest. You should always be able to see your baby's face without opening any of the fabric.

USING A CARRIER

A carrier is easier on your back than a sling as your baby gets heavier because his weight will be better supported. A soft cloth carrier can be used for a young baby, while a more substantial backpack with an aluminum frame is more suitable for an older baby. Most models enable you to hold your baby either facing inward close to your chest or facing forward.

Baby carriers are sold according to your baby's age or weight. They have stiff padding behind the head to give extra support to a young baby who doesn't yet have strong enough muscles to hold up his head on his own. Removable padding means you can use the carrier for an older baby facing forward.

Make sure you choose a carrier that is adjustable to suit both you and your partner.

For safety's sake, always put the carrier on and make sure it is securely fastened before you put your baby inside it; similarly, remove your baby from the carrier to a safe place before taking it off. (It's a good idea to be seated when you put your baby into and take him out of a carrier.)

TAKE CARE

It is very easy for a young baby to overheat inside a snug, padded carrier. Check every now and then that your baby is not sweating or in any discomfort.

Never leave your baby unattended in the carrier.

Don't use the carrier to transport your baby while you are driving.

Always protect your baby's head when you bend forward or to the side.

GETTING YOUR BABY INTO A CARRIER

1 **Put the carrier on first**
Following the manufacturer's instructions, fasten the straps and the buckles. When you feel comfortable and the carrier is secure, pick up your baby.

2 **Ease your baby inside** Sit down comfortably on a chair and open out the carrier. Holding your baby under his armpits, slowly lift him into the carrier.

3 **Adjust the straps** Once he's comfortably seated, check that your baby's weight is evenly distributed and adjust the straps as necessary.

Removing your baby from a carrier

When you are ready to take your baby out of the carrier, sit down, loosen the straps, then lift him out.

CALMING A CRYING BABY

During the first few weeks of life, crying is the only way your baby can communicate his needs. Most commonly, a baby cries because he is hungry but a number of other situations—discomfort, loneliness, and boredom—will trigger this response (see page 17). A regular caregiver will soon learn to recognize the different cries that can indicate the various causes, but sometimes your baby will cry for no discernible reason. This will no doubt upset and frustrate even the most confident parent, but don't take your baby's crying personally; simply comfort and reassure him with your presence.

Comfort station
When you respond to your baby's cries, you are letting him know that his needs matter to you and that they will be met. You won't be "spoiling" him.

It is important that you respond to your young baby's cries within a few minutes. The longer you leave your baby to cry, the more distressed he will become, making it more difficult for you to interpret the original source of his anxiety. Babies whose cries are ignored become non-responsive as they mature.

If your baby cries a lot and there are times when you find it hard to cope, ask your pediatrician for help.

Soothing ways

Although babies respond differently to the various soothing methods, here are a few things that might help you to calm your crying baby:

- Rock your baby against your shoulder or on your lap; this can calm even excitable babies.
- Rhythmic bottom patting, usually accompanied with a rocking motion, may prove relaxing.
- Use your voice to calm your baby. Your baby loves to hear your voice—humming, talking, or singing—but you may need to experiment to find the particular tone or pitch that best calms your baby.
- Swing your baby in a hammock or suspended baby seat. Alternatively, you could lie in a hammock with your baby in your arms and sway gently.
- Turn the lights down and introduce a low, monotonous sound such as the hum from a fan or household appliance.
- Offering a pacifier (see page 17) may help but it must always be kept sterile and it should never be sweetened or tied around your baby's neck.

CAUSES OF CRYING

Is he too hot or cold?
A young baby can quickly overheat or chill because his body's temperature control system takes months to become fully operational. Feel the back of his neck or his tummy. If he is too cold, add a layer. If too hot, remove a blanket or a layer of clothing.

Is he bored?
Your baby may need something to interest him. Even a small baby may stop crying if you give him a toy to play with or a mobile to distract him.

Is he lonely?
Most babies don't enjoy being separated from their parents. If you cannot constantly be in the same room as your baby, return frequently, turn on some gentle, soothing music or talk to him loudly so he knows you are nearby.

Is he overstimulated?
Too much activity surrounding your baby can be bewildering. Take him to a quiet room and soothe him by gently rocking him in your arms.

Offering a pacifier

Fretful babies are often comforted by sucking, so having a pacifier for short periods of time may soothe your baby. However, a pacifier is no substitute for your love and attention, so try to limit its use to calming stressful situations and before sleep.

EASING COLIC

Colic describes long episodes of crying unrelated to hunger or other common needs (see page 17). It is estimated that around 20 percent of babies suffer from it. During an attack, a previously contented baby suddenly brings her knees to her abdomen, clenches her fists, and begins screaming. Typically, these crying spells start at two to four weeks of age, gradually increase in duration and intensity, and peak at about six to eight weeks of age. If your baby howls the place down and seems inconsolable, by all means call your pediatrician. But if you're told "she's just got colic," caring physical contact is still the best way to ease her distress.

A great way to help to relieve your baby's anxiety is the "tiger in the tree" tummy massage (see page 19).

Possible causes

Nobody knows for sure why a baby gets colic; explanations include milk allergies, intestinal immaturity, wind, being overtired, fussy temperament, pressure on the infant's head during delivery, "bad bacteria" in the intestines, and parental inability to respond correctly to a baby's needs. None of these has been scientifically proven and colic is now thought to arise from not one but multiple possible causes (none of which has been definitely identified).

USING THE "TIGER IN THE TREE" MASSAGE

2 Cradle her tummy Place your right hand between your baby's knees, then open your palm and spread your fingers on her tummy. Tuck her right foot under your arm.

1 Pick up your baby Support your baby's front with your left arm, with her back resting against your body.

3 Knead her tummy Turning her so her weight is over your right hand, gently use your hand to knead her tummy.

SWADDLING YOUR BABY

Gently wrapping a baby in a lightweight blanket, sheet or shawl is an age-old technique that may soothe and comfort your infant. For some babies it becomes the trigger for sleep, but others don't enjoy it at all.

After spending the last months of her gestation being confined by your uterus, being able to freely move her arms and legs can come as quite a shock to your newborn. Through swaddling, you can help recreate your baby's former snug environment, making her feel safe and secure while she slowly adjusts to being in the outside world.

Your newborn has little control over her arms and legs and any sudden, jerky movements she makes can startle her and wake her from sleep. Swaddling can prevent this by keeping her limbs firmly wrapped. You should, however, keep at least one of her hands free if she likes to suck her fingers.

Swaddling can help babies to remain on their backs, a position for sleeping, which has been shown to reduce the risk of cot death or SIDS (see page 79).

A contented little baby
Many newborns find that being loosely wrapped in a lightweight covering prevents them from being disturbed by their own movements and lulls them into sleep.

TAKE CARE

Make sure your wrap is not too heavy and don't cover your baby's face with it, since that could cause her to overheat or interfere with her breathing. Beware of overheating your baby; the aim is to make her feel secure rather than keep her warm.

Don't wrap your baby too tightly; she should have room to wriggle.

Stop swaddling your baby once she is about a month old, because after that it can interfere with her mobility and development. When she begins to kick off the covers, it's a sign she no longer appreciates being wrapped up.

SWADDLING METHOD

1 **Place your baby on a blanket** Place a lightweight blanket on a flat surface and fold down one corner. Place your baby on it so her head is above the fold.

2 **Stretch the blanket across her body** Gently holding your baby's left arm by her side, stretch the left-hand corner of the blanket across her body and gently tuck it under her right arm. Then tuck the corner under her bottom.

4 **Tuck in the other end** Gently stretch the right-hand corner over and tuck it under your baby's bottom, leaving her hand free.

3 **Bring up the bottom of the blanket** Leaving room for your baby's legs to move freely, place the bottom of the blanket on her tummy.

FEEDING YOUR BABY

Whether breastfeeding, bottlefeeding, or giving your baby solids, the time that you spend feeding your baby should be special. If you are breastfeeding, you'll be able to feed your baby on demand without the need for extra equipment. If you decide to bottlefeed, you'll have to learn to make up infant formula and to keep your baby's feeding equipment scrupulously clean. Once you start introducing solids, you will want to make sure that the food you offer is healthy, and free from additives, excess salt, and sugar.

BREASTFEEDING

A mother's milk contains all the nutrients her baby needs to thrive for the first six months of life, as well as antibodies that help to build a strong immune system. Available on demand and at the right temperature, breast milk is also convenient. And breastfeeding fosters mutual love and intimacy between a mother and her baby.

Breastfeeding mothers usually regain their shape more quickly than bottlefeeding mothers because the hormone that stimulates milk production also makes the uterus contract, and this encourages your abdomen to return to its pre-birth size.

Demand feeding

Some mothers worry about breastfeeding: Are my breasts too small? Is my baby getting enough milk? Do I have enough milk? Milk is produced in the glands of the breasts, not in the fatty tissue, so breast size has no bearing on milk production. As long as you take your cues from your baby and feed on demand, your breasts will be stimulated to produce enough milk to satisfy his needs for nourishment. Be guided by his appetite rather than by a potentially restrictive schedule.

Feeding on demand depends entirely on your baby; some babies like to feel full all the time so may require feeding every one to two hours. Others may feed less frequently.

Pumping breast milk

If you cannot be there to breastfeed your baby or your breasts become overfull, you must express milk. This can be done by hand or with a pump.

With clean hands massage your breasts well. Gently stroke down toward the nipple and the areola, then place your thumbs above the areola and your fingers below. Develop a rhythmic motion of squeezing then pressing back toward your breastbone. After a few minutes, your milk should appear.

Pumps work on a suction principle; milk is squeezed from your breasts automatically.

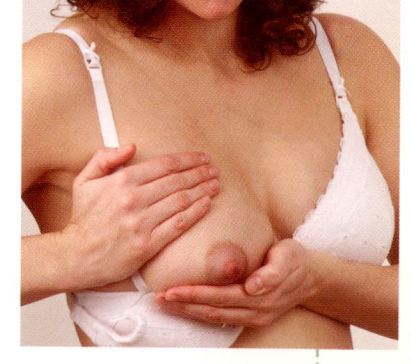

BREASTFEEDING YOUR BABY

1 **Encourage the rooting reflex**
Position your baby so that he is comfortably cradled in your arm with his mouth close to your nipple.

2 **Offer your nipple** Your baby's mouth should cover most of your areola, forming a tight seal.

3 **Check that he latches on properly** You should feel your baby's tongue pressing your nipple against the palate of his mouth and see his tongue and lower jaw milking your breast.

4 **Let him drink his fill** When there's no more milk, your baby will either drop off your breast or you may have to slip your little finger into the side of his mouth to break the suction. You can then offer your other breast.

BREASTFEEDING POSITIONS

Although many breastfeeding mothers sit upright on a low chair or with their backs propped up against furniture, there are times when feeding your baby lying down in bed will be more comfortable or convenient. While your baby is young, experiment with different positions so your baby doesn't insist on latching on in only one. It is a good idea, too, to change positions throughout the day to prevent undue soreness in one part of the breast.

Managing twins

Feeding both twins at once can make things easier. Newborns need frequent feeding at first, so feeding separately can mean almost continuous feeding/changing/settling without a break. Many twin babies eventually develop a preference for one breast over the other, so if you don't want this to occur, it is better to alternate your babies at each feed during the early weeks. Bear in mind, too, that many twins have unequal skills at breastfeeding, at least at first, so making sure each breast gets the stimulation of the better feeder is also a good idea. Creating a routine is easier when both babies are of a similar size and have similar feeding patterns. It can take up to six weeks to establish a routine, but once you have one, it will be much easier on you.

Feeding two at a time can be done in a number of ways— though the time to experiment is not when either of your babies is eager to be fed or when they're sleepy. You may find that a position that didn't work when your twins were new becomes easier when they're older.

The most popular positions include the football (each baby is positioned under one of your arms with her legs tucked behind your back) and parallel (both babies are held against your chest with their heads facing in the same direction) holds. Another common position is to hold them in a V shape with their feet either touching or crossed over each other. Special V-shaped feeding pillows are available, which support each baby's head and shoulders leaving your hands and forearms free.

Holds for twins

The most popular positions include (left to right) the V shape, parallel, and football holds.

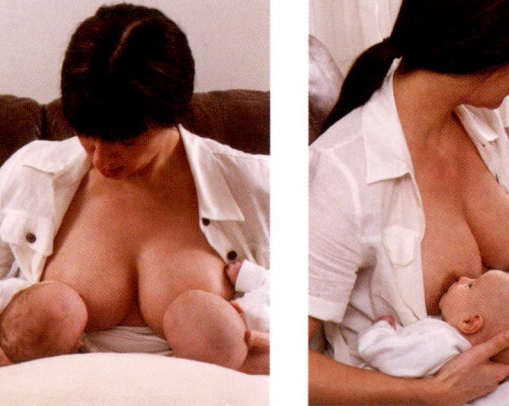
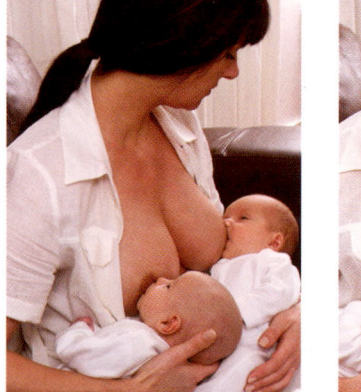

POSITIONS FOR A SINGLETON

Lying side-by-side
With plenty of pillows to prop you up, place your baby in the crook of your elbow with her mouth in line with your nipple.

Football hold
Position your baby under one of your arms so that her legs are tucked behind your back and her head can be supported with the hand on that side.

Parallel hold
Hold your baby along your chest and support her head and back with one hand.

BOTTLEFEEDING

Whether you or your partner bottlefeed your baby, it's possible to come close to the intimacy of breastfeeding: sit comfortably in a chair or on the sofa with plenty of cushions for support. Keep distractions to a minimum; try unplugging the phone or having older children occupied in another room. Play some music to help you relax and enjoy the occasion. You may like to bottlefeed topless so your baby can feel and smell your skin while he feeds.

Formula milk takes longer to digest than breast milk so you won't have to feed your baby as frequently as you would if you were breastfeeding. Babies should be fed on demand and most newborns will need feeding every two hours, although this can vary in accordance with your baby's particular needs. After about one month, your baby may require feeding every three hours, and by two to three months of age, he may only need feeding every four hours. As your baby matures, his sucking ability increases, and he will be able to consume milk at a faster rate.

Nipples come with different hole sizes so choose one appropriate to your baby's age and check the hole size regularly.

It's recommended to always start feeding with a freshly made up bottle of milk each time. Never refrigerate and then reheat a previously warmed bottle.

If you are bottlefeeding your baby with expressed breast milk, it's best that the milk is fresh: it can be left at room temperature (up to 76°F) for between four and six hours or refrigerated (32–39°F), then warmed up if necessary (see box right).

Warming milk

Most parents prefer to warm bottled milk to make it more closely resemble breast milk. Most babies, however, don't mind it being cooler, say at room temperature rather than cold. Do not give a baby milk that has been left for over an hour—bacteria multiply quickly in warm temperatures.

A special time
Feeding your bottlefed baby skin to skin helps ensure the experience is as satisfying and intimate as breastfeeding.

BOTTLEFEEDING YOUR BABY

1 **Elicit the rooting reflex** If you stroke his cheek, your baby will automatically turn his head toward you with his mouth open, ready to suck.

Check temperature

Test the temperature of the milk before giving it to your baby by shaking a few drops on to the inside of your wrist. It should feel warm, not hot.

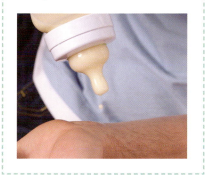

2 **Insert the nipple into your baby's mouth** Angle the bottle at about 45 degrees so that the neck of the bottle is full of milk and there are no air bubbles. Place the nipple into your baby's mouth. Make sure the nipple does not slip about in your baby's mouth, preventing proper sucking. Hold the bottle steady and adjust the angle of the bottle so that the top is always full of milk.

3 **Remove the bottle** When your baby has finished, or you want to remove the bottle to burp him, slip your little finger into the side of his mouth to break the suction and slide the nipple out.

CLEANING BOTTLES

If you choose to bottlefeed your baby it is important for your baby's health that you maintain a high standard of cleanliness. Milk is the perfect breeding ground for bacteria, and if you are not careful, your baby could suffer stomach pains and fail to put on weight at a crucial time of her development.

All feeding equipment—bottles, nipples, rings, discs, and caps—must be kept scrupulously clean by being washed in a dishwasher. If you have chlorinated tap water, wash the utensils with dishwashing detergent in hot tap water, then rinse with hot tap water. If you don't have chlorinated tap water, boil your utensils in water for five to 10 minutes to sterilize them. Sterilizing can change the shape of nipples, particularly the hole size, so make sure you check them frequently.

All new bottles and related equipment should be sterilized before using them with your baby.

Your young baby will be using up to eight bottles a day but as she gets older, she will need fewer bottles, which will make your workload easier.

Out and about

You will have more than enough to think about on an outing without having to worry about filling your baby's bottles. Make life a little easier by using cartons of ready-to-feed formula, or take a measured amount of boiled water in a sealed flask and pre-measured formula in a sterile container.

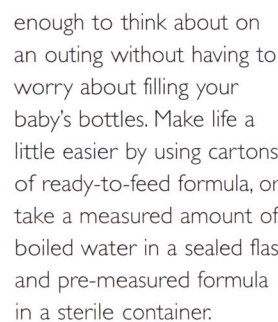

Boiling method
You don't need special sterilizing equipment—though it can make life easier. You simply submerge bottles, rings, discs, and caps in boiling water for 5–10 minutes and let them cool with the lid on. Nipples will degrade in boiling water over time.

HANDWASH METHOD

1 **Wash bottles and rings** Place bottles and rings in warm, soapy water. Use a bottle brush around the rings and on the screw thread at the top of the bottles and on the necks where hardened milk can easily get stuck. Rinse thoroughly.

2 **Wash nipples** Clean the surface, then turn the nipples inside out and scrub them using a nipple brush to ensure that you remove any stubborn milk particles. Rinse thoroughly.

Fitting a nipple

To fit a nipple into the screw ring, hold it with freshly washed tongs and pull it through.

MAKING UP FORMULA

Formula milk is usually based on cow's milk and it contains all the vitamins and minerals your baby needs for the first six months. Powdered formula is the most popular choice, although liquid-concentrate and ready-made forms (in cartons and bottles) are also available. Ready-made formula is more expensive, but can be convenient for night-time feeds and when you are out and about with your baby. When buying, make sure formula is within its sell-by date, and that containers are free of bulges, dents, leaks, or rust spots; formula in a damaged container may be unsafe.

There are a few basic rules to follow when preparing powdered formula. The most important is to always make sure your hands and all the equipment you use are clean. Follow the manufacturer's measurements to the letter, as they are calculated to suit your baby's needs exactly. Make up individual bottles as you need them, although once a baby is about a month old, most parents make up enough bottles for a day. While it's best to feed your baby freshly made-up formula, prepared formula can be refrigerated for up to 24 hours while an opened can of ready-to-feed formula or prepared bottles using the same, can be stored in the fridge for up to 48 hours. Unfinished formula should be discarded within an hour after serving your baby. Formula can be offered warm, cold, or at room temperature.

Baby milks

All baby milks marketed in the US have to contain certain levels of protein, carbohydrate, fats, vitamins, and minerals. A special brand may be prescribed if your baby was premature, or has a feeding or medical problem. Soy-based formulas, which contain no cow's milk proteins, may be prescribed for babies who have an allergic reaction to cow's milk formula or if there is a strong history of allergy in their families. However, don't start on or change to non-dairy baby milks without first talking to your pediatrician.

Formula choice
Deciding which formula to use is something you can discuss with your pediatrician It should be a brand that you can buy easily and locally. If your baby is colicky or you think he may be having a reaction to the formula, consult your pediatrician.

MAKING UP A BOTTLE

1 **Add water to a bottle** If your tap water is "safe," use room-temperature tap water otherwise bring cold water to a rolling boil for one minute only then cool to room temperature for no more than 30 minutes before using.

2 **Measure the formula** Use the scoop provided with the formula to measure the required amount. Level off any excess powder using the device in the container or a knife. Do not pat down.

3 **Add the formula to the water and mix** Double check the recommended number of scoops of formula and add to the bottle. Screw a clean nipple on to the bottle then cover with a cap. Shake the bottle hard so that water and powder are thoroughly mixed.

Preparing liquid concentrate

Wash and thoroughly rinse the top of the formula can before opening. Measure the amount of concentrate you need and pour it into a clean bottle. Then add water as indicated. Place the nipple and retaining ring on the bottle and cover with a cap. Shake the bottle hard so that water and concentrate are thoroughly mixed.

TAKE CARE

Never heap or pack a scoop of formula or add an extra one, and make sure the amount of water is correct. If the formula is too concentrated, it may make your baby dehydrated; if it's too weak, your baby won't get enough nourishment. To make extra formula, always add more water and powder (or concentrate) in the correct proportions.

BURPING YOUR BABY

Whether you breastfeed or bottlefeed your baby, he may take in air along with the milk he ingests. This air can form bubbles in his stomach and may cause discomfort as well as a feeling of fullness. If your baby's stomach hurts, he may cry (see Calming a crying baby, pages 16–17). If he feels full, he probably won't continue feeding but will be hungry again very soon. It may help to try and get your baby to expel this accumulated air.

Breastfed babies are able to make a tighter seal around their mother's nipples than bottlefed babies around a bottle's teat, so it is usually sufficient to burp a breastfed baby after he has finished each breast.

A bottlefed baby may need to be burped more often—after every few ounces. Don't interrupt a feed to burp your baby, however; you should wait until your baby pauses naturally.

Bibs

While being fed, or just after, it is quite common for babies to spit up some milk. It is a good idea, therefore, to protect your baby's clothes with a bib, and your own clothes with a cloth or cloth diaper. A basic toweling bib is all that's required until you start weaning your baby.

Enjoy this special time
Feeding is just as much about emotional nourishment as it is about meeting your baby's nutritional needs. Take this time to relax with your baby, to communicate your love. and establish a special rapport.

BURPING POSITIONS

Spitting up and reflux

It's quite common for a baby to spit up some milk while being burped. Because the back of the throat and the top of the stomach are very close to each other, some babies regurgitate a little milk alongside each burp. This is perfectly normal and nothing to worry about. Some infants, however, particularly those born prematurely, may regurgitate their stomach contents —although the amount brought up is usually far less than they take in. Known medically as reflux, this can be helped by holding your baby in an upright position for 20 minutes after each feed. Regurgitation will happen less and less as your baby grows, so if he is otherwise content and gaining weight normally, there's nothing to worry about.

On your shoulder

Lift your baby up so that his head is over your shoulder and facing away from your neck. Use one hand to support his bottom and the other to gently rub or pat his back.

Across your knees

Lay your baby down so that his tummy rests on one knee and his chest on your other knee or in the crook of your elbow. His head should face away from you and his mouth should be unobstructed. Gently rub or pat his back with one or both hands.

Sitting up

Gently raise your baby into a sitting position on your lap. Support his head with one hand while you use the other hand to gently rub or pat around his shoulder blades.

FEEDING YOUR BABY SOLIDS

The American Academy of Pediatrics recommends waiting until your baby is four to six months old before being given solids. Until your baby is a year old, however, you should still continue to give her breast or formula milk. Your pediatrician will be able to give you more specific advice on how and when to start.

Introducing your baby to solids will be a big step in her development so start slowly, at first, one or two new tastes every few days will suffice Once your baby is happy with these, you can introduce more new foods and eventually start mixing different foods together. Don't try to force your baby to eat something she obviously dislikes; wait a week or two and then try again.

Make sure you sterilize your feeding spoon and bowl before use and protect your baby's clothes with a substantial bib. It may take a few weeks for your baby to master the technique of taking food from a spoon.

Commercial baby foods

Although many moms prefer home-made meals, it can be helpful to have some jars of prepared food on hand when you need them.
- Check the labels to ensure the ingredients are suitable for your baby's age.
- Check the expiry date and that the seals have not been broken.
- Avoid foods that contain gluten, nuts, seeds, eggs, fish, citrus fruits and juices, honey, and added sugar.

Let her experiment!
Babies are messy eaters, but by using her fingers, your baby can find out all about the texture of her food as well as its taste, and improve her hand-eye coordination. So, although eating with fingers is messier, your baby will actually learn valuable lessons.

FEEDING YOUR BABY SOLIDS

Beginning solids

At first you will simply want to introduce a couple of spoonfuls of infant cereal along with your baby's regular supply of milk before moving on to smoothly puréed vegetables or fruits, Infant cereal (rice, oatmeal, or barley) is fortified with needed iron. Your baby will still get most of her essential nutrients from milk. Over time, the amount of solids you offer and that your baby takes in will gradually reduce your baby's need for nourishment from milk.

Try a wide range of foods but introduce them slowly. Wait a few days after each new food to check for any negative reaction. Your baby will probably prefer blander foods to start with, so avoid strong, spicy tastes.

Spoonfeeding

Hold your baby in an upright position in your lap or, if she's able to support her back and neck (generally, about six months of age), sit her in a highchair. Scoop up some of the purée on a long-handled, soft feeding spoon and put it just between her lips so that she can suck the food off. Be careful not to put the spoon too far in her mouth as she may gag. Some of the food will probably reappear until she gets used to taking it off the spoon.

First foods

The texture of your baby's food should keep pace with her progress. Start by puréeing food to an almost liquid consistency (like heavy cream), then gradually process for a shorter time in the blender so the food is lumpier. From here, you can mash, grind, or finely chop the ingredients.

Smooth purée

Chunky purée

Chopped chicken

HELPING YOUR BABY TO FEED HIMSELF

Once your baby has learned to take food from a spoon he will want to start feeding himself. He'll enjoy gnawing on finger foods when his teeth start to come through, or trying to get food from the bowl into his mouth using his fingers or a spoon. As his hand-mouth coordination improves, he will be able to start drinking from a cup (open-top, lidded or sippy).

It's important to make sure mealtimes are enjoyable. The best time to feed yur baby is when he's well rested and not fussy. If meals are fun, this will encourage your baby to enjoy himself and promote a healthy attitude towards food in the future. Moreover, success with self-feeding will not only give your baby confidence, but will allow him to join other family members at the dinner table which will promote his sociability.

What babies need

Carbohydrate/starchy foods
(about 3–4 servings a day)
These are excellent sources of energy, vitamins, minerals, and fiber (but avoid giving too many high-fiber foods to babies as they find them difficult to digest and they can upset the digestive system):
- Sugar-free breakfast cereals and oats
- Pasta and noodles
- Rice
- Bread
- Potatoes

Protein foods
(about 2–3 servings a day)
Protein is essential for growth and repair in the body. Offer a combination of protein foods to get a good mix of essential amino acids:
- Fish (make sure there are no bones)
- Tofu
- Meat and poultry
- Meat alternatives
- Well-cooked eggs
- Full-fat cheese (grated or cubed)
- Beans and lentils

Milk
Milk provides protein, vitamins, and minerals, particularly calcium for strong teeth and bones. Cow's milk can be used in cooking from six months but not as a drink until your baby is one year old, when full-fat milk can be introduced. Semi-skimmed milk is suitable from two years, while skimmed milk is not recommended until five years of age, as it does not provide the energy a growing child requires.

Fruit and vegetables
(3–4 or more servings a day)
Fresh, frozen, canned (in natural juice or water), and dried fruit and vegetables are an essential part of a baby's diet. They make ideal first foods and provide rich amounts of vitamins, minerals, and fiber. Try to provide your baby with a variety of fresh produce. The following are all suitable but the list is far from exhaustive:
- Peeled apple
- Banana
- Mango
- Apricots
- Peaches and nectarines
- Melon
- Strawberries
- Carrot
- Broccoli
- Green beans
- Peas
- Pepper
- Snap peas

SELF-FEEDING ESSENTIALS

Finger foods

Offer steamed vegetables such as diced carrots, sweet potato chunks, or broccoli florets; cooked pasta shapes; o-shaped cereal or rice cakes. Avoid giving nuts, fruit with seeds, unpeeled fruit that has a hard skin, and pieces of food that are too small. They may cause your baby to choke.

Trainer cups

Unbreakable plastic feeding cups with weighted bases and double handles are recommended when weaning your baby off the bottle. Some pediatricians recommended open tops, others tight-fitting lids with integral or changeable spouts. Your baby should start with water or diluted, unsweetened fruit juice.

Spoon or fingers

Your baby may grab hold of your spoon to feed himself or may prefer to use his hands instead of utensils. Let him have his own spoon and if you get the chance, swap an empty one for one with food on it. You can help your baby by offering foods that are easy to scoop up on a spoon like mashed potato, thick cottage cheese, cooked rice, and cereal.

CHANGING YOUR BABY'S DIAPER

Your newborn baby will urinate as many as 20 times a day in the first few weeks, so you will spend a lot of your time changing her diaper. When you change your baby make sure you have everything you need by your side—fresh diaper, wipes or cotton balls and water, and, if using disposables, a sack in which to put the dirty diaper . Being prepared means your baby alone won't be wet and exposed for long. Never leave your baby unattended on a raised surface; she could easily roll right off. Always clean your baby thoroughly at each change (see pages 54–55) and make sure you wash your hands afterward.

DISPOSABLE DIAPERS

Disposables are currently the most popular choice for parents because they are convenient and easy to use. You don't have to wash them or worry about pins, liners, or plastic pants. However, they are expensive—particularly if you plan to have more children—and many people worry about their impact on the environment. Make sure the diaper you use fits snugly around your baby's thighs. Adjust the waist so that you can fit one finger between your baby's tummy and the diaper.

Watch out!

A baby boy may be stimulated to urinate by the feel of air on his skin, so keep a spare diaper handy to cover his penis, just in case.

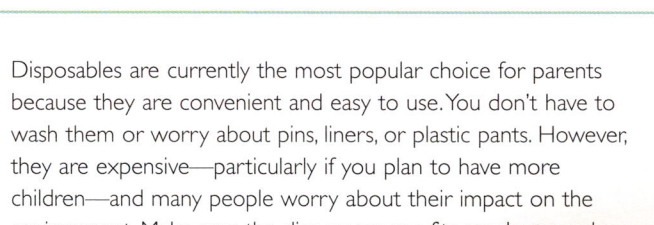

PUTTING ON A DISPOSABLE

1 **Open out the diaper and place it under your baby's bottom** Lay your baby on her back on a changing mat or other flat surface. Lift her legs up by the ankles and slide an opened diaper under her bottom.

2 **Bring the front up between her legs** Let go of her ankles and place the opened-out front of the diaper across her tummy. (Make sure a boy's penis points downward or he may urinate into the waistband.)

3 **Fasten the sides** Smooth the diaper over her tummy. Bring one side into the middle, unpeel the protective backing to the tab, and stick down. Repeat with the other side. Fold the top of the diaper in neatly against her tummy.

TAKING OFF A DISPOSABLE

1 **First unfasten the sides** Unpeel the tabs from each side of the diaper. Take the front of the diaper down between your baby's legs.

2 **Use the diaper to clean any mess** Use the front of the diaper to wipe your baby's bottom clean of any excrement.

3 **Roll up and remove** Fold the sides in toward the middle, roll the diaper up. and slide it from under your baby's bottom. Retape the rolled-up bundle and put it in a diaper sack.

REUSEABLE DIAPERS

Cloth diapers can be made from cotton, bamboo, microfiber, or hemp, and need to be rinsed, sanitized, washed, and dried. In addition to fine muslin squares for a newborn and standard square cotton or terrycloth ones for an older baby, most modern cloth diapers are either pre-shaped with a waterproof covering or consist of pads, wraps, and liners.

Fitted diapers come already tailored to fit a baby's bottom, so you don't have to fold them or fiddle about with diaper pins. Most have elasticated legs and waist, as well as self-stick tabs or snap fastenings. All-in-ones have a waterproof cover. It's also possible to buy diapers with a waterproof outer layer and a fleecy inner layer. These layers form a pocket into which an absorbent insert is placed to soak up the wetness so the fleece dries quickly and acts as a stay-dry layer next to a baby's skin.

Cloth diapers should be pre-washed before use but avoid fabric softeners as these can make them less absorbent. You also should check and follow the care label.

Wraps or covers

Waterproof or water-resistant covers that go over separate absorbent diapers are available; these fasten over the diaper with Velcro® or snaps.

Wraps can be made from a number of fabrics. The cheapest are usually made from plastic but are not as comfortable or durable as polyester bonded to a urethane laminate (PUL), which is waterproof but has the soft, comfortable feel of fabric on the outside. Polyester fleece and wool wraps are also available although they are not waterproof.

Check the care label for washing instructions; many shouldn't be sanitized.

Liners

Some contemporary diaper "systems" depend on a fleecy liner, which is reused but one-way liners can make life easier with all diapers. They draw urine away from the skin to help keep your baby's skin drier and prevent excrement soiling the fabric. Paper liners are made from recycled paper and are biodegradable. Used ones should be flushed down the toilet or placed on the compost heap. Fleece liners need to be washed (see pages 44–45).

PUTTING ON A FITTED DIAPER

1 **Prepare diaper and place baby on top** Open out the diaper and, if necessary, insert a pad. For an older baby, you may want to use a liner. Place on a changing mat then put your baby on the diaper, aligning his waist with the top.

2 **Bring the front of the diaper up between his legs** Pull the front of the diaper taut and bring it up between your baby's legs. The diaper should fit snugly, but not too tightly, around your baby's thighs.

3 **Fasten the sides** Bring one side over and fasten it with the self-stick tab or snap fastening. Repeat on the other side. If the diaper is not fitting your baby's tummy snugly enough, undo and refasten the sides.

Taking off a fitted diaper

Unfasten the diaper and lower the front between your baby's legs. If there is any mess, hold your baby's ankles with one hand, raising his bottom, and use the front edge of the fabric to wipe away any excrement. With your baby's bottom still raised, fold the sides of the diaper into the middle and slide the diaper out from underneath his bottom, rolling it up as you remove it.

FOLDED CLOTH DIAPERS

In certain circumstances, a properly folded cloth diaper will better contain urine and excrement than a disposable or a fitted diaper. A cloth diaper also allows more air to circulate around your baby's bottom so the chances of skin irritation and diaper rash are reduced.

Cloth diapers generally are made of 100 percent cotton so are not waterproof by themselves; you will need to use a wrap or some plastic pants on top. Terrycloth diapers are the most absorbent but also the bulkiest, although flatter-weave versions are also available. Cloth diapers and wraps or plastic pants will make your baby's bottom a few sizes bigger, so keep this in mind when you are shopping for baby clothes.

Cloth diapers can be folded in a variety of ways to suit the shape and size of your baby. A popular fold for a young baby is the kite fold (see right). This produces a neat shape and is very absorbent but it needs two pins. You can adjust the size by varying the depth of the last fold.

Kite fold

Place the diaper in front of you. Bring two adjoining sides into the center to produce a kite shape.

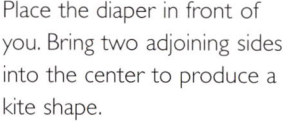

Take the point at the top of the kite and neatly fold it down into the middle. (This is where your baby's waist will be positioned.)

Take the point at the bottom of the kite and bring it to the middle. (This fold will be brought up between your baby's legs.) You can adjust the depth of this fold to make the surface area larger or smaller.

FOLDED DIAPER

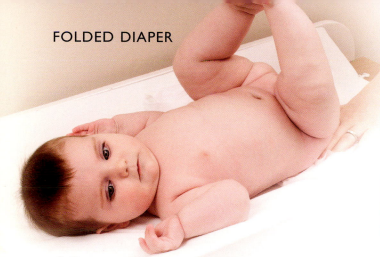

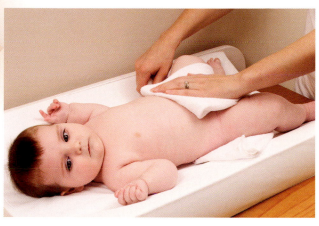

1 **Place your baby on the diaper** Fold the cloth square as shown on page 42. Lower your baby on to the diaper; her waist should align with the top edge.

2 **Bring the diaper up between your baby's legs** Gather the corners of the cloth in your hands and pull it up between her legs, smoothing the front over her tummy.

3 **Pin the sides and cover** Keeping your hand between the cloth and your baby's skin, pin one side. Adjust the fit, then fasten a second pin on the other side. Open out a wrap, slide it under your baby's bottom, and secure it over the diaper or slip a pair of open plastic pants under her bottom and up between her legs. Make sure the diaper is well tucked inside.

Taking off a folded cloth diaper

Lay your baby on a changing mat; undo the wrap or slip off the plastic pants. Place your hand between the fabric and your baby's skin and carefully unfasten each pin; place them out of your baby's reach. Slowly lower the diaper and if there is any mess, hold your baby's ankles with one hand, raising her bottom, and use the front edge of the fabric to wipe away any excrement. With your baby's bottom still raised, fold the sides of the diaper into the middle and slide it out from underneath her bottom, rolling it up as you remove it.

CARING FOR SOILED DIAPERS

Sanitizing, wash,ing and drying diapers, liners, and wraps can be a laborious process. To minimize the fuss, make sure that you are well organized beforehand. Incomplete cleaning can leave waste ammonia or bacteria on diapers, either of which can lead to diaper rash and infection. Using too much detergent on diapers, on the other hand, will irritate your baby's sensitive skin. Therefore, measure the amount of sanitizing fluid and detergents carefully and rinse everything twice.

Sanitizing methods

You can sanitize your diapers by soaking them in a bleach-free chemical solution, or by washing them at 60°C. Chemical methods involve using a diaper pail and mesh bag; an alternative to chemicals is a couple of drops of tea tree oil (a powerful natural antiseptic) or lavender oil. Although it's not strictly necessary, some parents prefer to store urine-soaked and soiled diapers separately.

If you choose to sanitize by washing at 60°C, you can simply store your diapers in a dry bucket. Or, you can store them in a water-filled bucket sprinkled with some baking soda to reduce odors. However, shake soiled fleece liners and diapers into the toilet bowl to remove as much excrement as possible, then rinse them. If there is a lot of soiling, hold them by the corner in the toilet bowl and flush, or sluice in a diaper pail filled with water.

When you have a full load of diapers, wraps, and liners, put them into your washing machine. (A mesh bag can make this a little easier.) It is a good idea to do a rinse cycle to remove any excess soiling and urine before running the wash cycle. Wash at 60°C using half to two-thirds of the recommended amount of non-biological detergent (don't use a product containing chlorine bleach or whitener). Every so often, when you have time, you could do an extra final rinse to remove any built-up detergent residues from the diapers.

Diaper mesh

This is a perforated sack that holds dirty diapers, liners, and wraps in a pail, and can be placed as is in the washing machine.

WASHING SOILED DIAPERS

1 **Sit the mesh bag in a diaper pail** Hook the open top over the pail rim. Add used diapers, wraps, and liners.

2 **Remove the bag and contents** When ready to wash, lift off the bag and its contents from the rim.

3 **Wash at 60°C** Open out the mesh bag or turn out the contents into the washer and put all items through a cycle.

4 **Take out of the machine and dry** If you've placed an opened out bag in the machine, the contents will work free. Remove all items from the machine and dry.

Drying diapers, wraps, and liners

Air drying is ideal when the weather permits and holders that hook over a washing line are readily available. You can also dry everything in a tumble dryer. The best alternative to air drying is to hang items or place on a rack or airer in a warm place where air can circulate freely. Avoid placing items directly on a radiator as this can harden certain materials.

DRESSING YOUR BABY

Young babies generally don't like being dressed or undressed as they dislike the feeling of air on their skin and garments being placed over their heads. Dress and undress your baby somewhere warm, have everything ready, and be prepared to work quickly—you should never leave your baby alone on a raised surface, whether or not he can roll over. For clothing, natural fabrics like cotton and wool will be warm and also allow your baby's skin to breathe, but avoid scratchy materials. Always wash your baby's clothes before first use with a non-biological powder.

UNDERSHIRTS

Your baby's ability to regulate his own body temperature is not fully functional for the first few months of his life. As a result, he can very easily become too hot or too cold. Unless it is very warm, always dress your baby in an undershirt. In very hot weather, he may wear just an undershirt and a diaper.

Undershirt designs vary, but most have wide, loose necks to make them easy to put on and prevent your baby from becoming distressed by having material dragged over his face. Models that join at the crotch with snaps won't ride up so will keep your baby warmer and more comfortable.

PUTTING ON AN UNDERSHIRT

1 Place the shirt behind his head Using both hands, gather the material to the neck and stretch the opening wide. Gently raise your baby's head and slip the shirt over his head and neck.

3 Straighten the shirt Gently smooth the fabric down over his back and front and, if applicable, fasten the snaps between his legs. Take care not to pinch his skin.

2 Adjust fabric and locate sleeve Straighten the fabric around your baby's neck. Take hold of one sleeve and gather up the material. Insert your hand through the sleeve and grasp your baby's wrist. With your free hand, gently ease the sleeve over his arm. Repeat with the other sleeve.

Taking off an undershirt

Work in reverse by freeing your baby's arms and then easing the shirt over his head. Gather each sleeve up in one hand and use your other hand to gently guide your baby's arm out of the sleeve. Concertina the material at your baby's neck and, using both hands, stretch the opening of the neck as wide as possible then slip the undershirt over the front, then the back, of your baby's head.

Removing a dirty undershirt Free your baby's arms, as above, then concertina the material at the neck and bring it through his legs, up his back and down the front of his body—to prevent his face coming in contact with urine or fecal matter.

ONESIES

An all-in-one sleepsuit is a staple of most babies' wardrobes. It is easy to put on and take off, and covers the whole body, including the feet, so that you don't need to bother with socks or bootees.

When buying aa onesie, choose one that is colorfast and soft—natural fibers are always best. Since babies vary widely in their rates of growth, use your baby's height and weight—rather than age—as a guide when selecting clothes.

If you have a choice, go for looser, baggier suits that will give your baby a bit of growing space and room to move. Pay particular attention to the neck, which should be loose and should not constrict your baby's movement in any way.

Onesies make changing easy: they are easy to undo and take off, and you can change your baby in stages so that she doesn't get upset by being completely undressed.

If you are only changing her diaper, leave the top of the suit on while you attend to her bottom. If a full change of clothing is needed, attend to her bottom, then slip a clean garment on to her bottom half before removing the top half of the dirty suit.

PUTTING ON A ONESIE

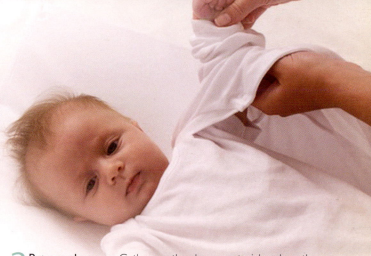

1 **Put the feet and legs on** Open out the suit on a non-slip surface and lay your baby on top of it. Gather up the material of one leg and slide it over your baby's foot, making sure her toes go all the way in. Smooth the material up her leg. Repeat for the other foot.

2 **Put one sleeve on** Gather up the sleeve material and gently slide it over your baby's wrist, making certain that her fingers and nails don't get caught in the fabric.

3 **Cover her arm and shoulder** Slide the material up her arm and over her shoulder. Pull on the material instead of her arm. Now put on the other sleeve. If the sleeves are too long, fold the cuffs back so her hands are free.

4 **Join the snaps** Adjust the suit so the two sides meet in the center. Align the snaps. Starting at the crotch and working up, do up the snaps. Make sure you join the crotch snaps correctly as it's easy to make a mistake.

Taking off a onesie

Open all the snaps. One at a time, support her knees while you gently ease the material away from her legs. If you're going to remove the suit, lift your baby's legs while you gently push it up under her back to the shoulders. Then hold your baby's elbows while you gather up the sleeve and gently ease it away from her wrists.

OUTDOOR WEAR

It's important that your baby is neither too hot nor too cold. As a guide, your baby needs about the same number of layers that you are wearing. You can more easily ensure that you can control her temperature by reducing or increasing the layers as necessary, so several thin garments are better than one thick one. Premature or small-for-dates babies need an extra layer. Bear in mind, too, that a sling or carrier counts as a layer of clothing.

In hot weather, your baby may only need an undershirt and a diaper, or perhaps just a diaper. In mild, but not hot, weather a cotton cardigan over a onesie is ideal. In cold weather, she will need a cardigan over her onesie and a hat. Choose a flat-textured cardigan made of non-fuzzy fibers with a zipper or large buttons as this will prevent your baby's fingers getting caught and will be easier to put on. Natural fibers such as cotton and wool will keep your baby warm without making her sweat. For really cold weather, a flannel snowsuit with a hood is a good option and can be put on just as you would a onesie (see page 49).

You can check if your baby is warm enough by placing your (warm) hand under her undershirt to feel her chest or back; she should feel a little warmer than your hand.

Hats

In the cooler months, a hat is essential. Your baby should wear a lightweight one most of the time and a heavier one when your head feels a little cold. In the summer, a sunhat is essential.

Basic wardrobe

2–3 undershirts

4 pairs socks

6 onesies

2 hats

2 cardigans

2–3 bibs

1 snowsuit
(for cold weather)

2 pairs each scratch mittens
and cold weather mittens

PUTTING ON A CARDIGAN

1 **Put one sleeve on**
Sit your baby on your lap facing forward. Gather up one sleeve in your hands and guide it over your baby's hand and up her arm until you can ease it over her shoulder.

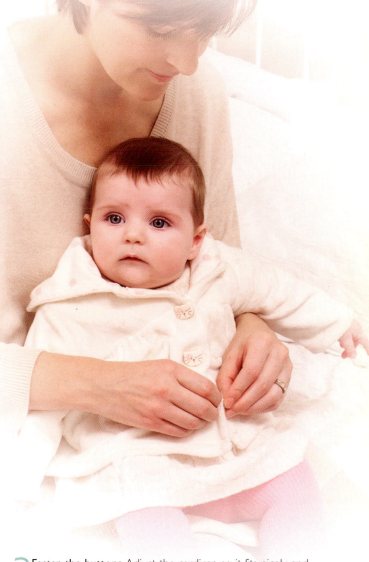

2 **Put the second sleeve on** Gently bring the cardigan around your baby's back. Gather up the other sleeve in your hand and place it over her hand then bring it gently up her arm to her shoulder.

3 **Fasten the buttons** Adjust the cardigan so it fits nicely and the buttons are aligned. Do up the buttons starting at the neck end.

KEEPING YOUR BABY CLEAN

A newborn has very sensitive skin and a limited potential for getting dirty, so "topping and tailing" is often all you need to do. Some doctors recommend that babies shouldn't be bathed until the umbilical cord stump has fallen off and a circumcision has healed.

Once you feel confident about giving your baby a bath, you'll find it easier to wash him using a bath support or in a baby bath. Make sure the room is warm and that you have a soft, fluffy towel ready to wrap him in as soon as you've finished.

SPONGE BATH

A simple sponge bath is all your young baby needs most days, since only his exposed areas—face, neck creases, hands, and feet—and genitals and bottom are likely to become dirty.

It's a good idea to undress your baby a little bit at a time, and wrap him up in the towel to keep him warm, redressing him as you finish wiping and drying each area.

Use a clean cotton ball, washcloth, or soft sponge and cooled, boiled water for every area. Do not use tap water (although you can when your baby is older) as you will be cleaning your baby's eyes, or talcum powder or soap as they will further dry his very sensitive skin. Equally, avoid cleaning inside your baby's nose or ears; his inner surfaces are lined with mucous membranes that clean themselves; interfering with them will do your baby more harm than good.

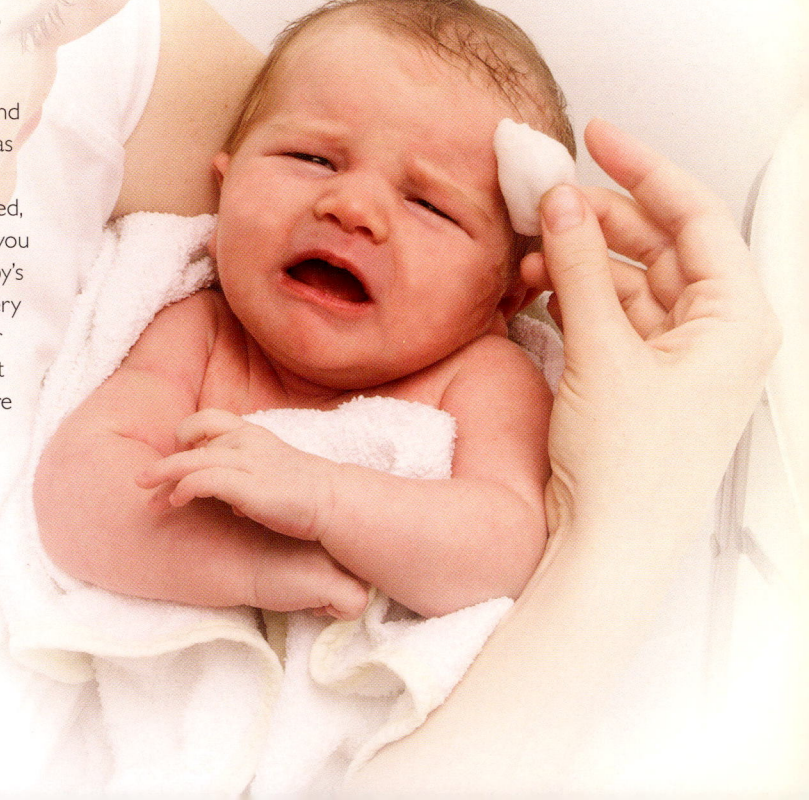

"TOPPING AND TAILING" YOUR BABY

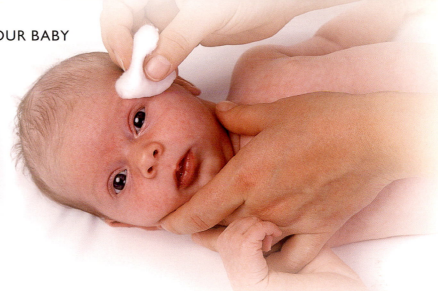

1 **Your baby's eyes** Using cooled, boiled water, wet a cotton ball and wipe from the inner to the outer corner of his eye. Use a fresh cotton ball for the other eye to prevent transferring infections. Use more cotton balls to wipe around and behind—but not inside—his ears.

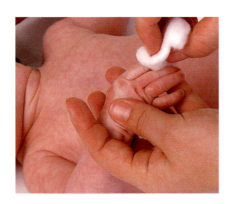

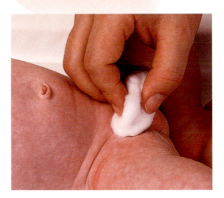

2 **Hands and fingers** Use more cotton balls, or a washcloth or soft sponge to clean his hands, unclenching them to check for sharp fingernails and dirt between the fingers. Pat dry with a soft towel or cloth.

3 **Feet and toes** Wipe the top and bottom of your baby's feet, and between his toes. They may be tightly curled so gently ease them apart. Again, pat dry with a towel.

4 **Tummy and legs** Holding down your baby's legs firmly but gently, wipe his tummy area. Use fresh cotton balls or a clean area of the washcloth to wipe along his leg folds. Wipe downward and away from your baby's body (particularly with a girl) to avoid transferring any infections to the genital area.

CLEANING YOUR BABY'S BOTTOM

Probably your most frequent task of the day, changing your baby's diaper often involves cleaning her bottom and the surrounding area—particularly if a diaper was soiled.

Diaper rash

A baby's skin is very sensitive and most babies experience at least some minor diaper rash from time to time. Although you can successfully treat this condition at home, it is always best to try and prevent it.

Diaper rash is mainly caused by prolonged contact with urine and feces, so the best way to prevent it is to change your baby's diaper as soon as it's wet or soiled.

The first signs of diaper rash may be a mild red patch or small bumps on the buttocks. The skin may be angry-looking and moist, with spots or blisters around the buttocks or between the legs.

If your baby does have a rash, clean the area gently but thoroughly and apply a diaper rash cream. If the rash doesn't clear up with ordinary creams and the skin is bright red with white or red pimples in the folds, it may be infected with thrush, a fungal infection. In this case, consult your pediatrician.

Air bathing

Exposing your baby's bottom to the air occasionally—say at diaper change time—will not only help heal diaper rash but may also prevent it. Put a towel on the floor and let your baby kick for a while.

Caring for a circumcised boy

If your baby boy has been circumcised, avoid giving him a bath until the wound has healed. If he has a dressing, you may need to apply a new one when you change his diaper for the first day or two. Use a light dressing such as gauze and put petroleum jelly on the gauze so that it won't stick to his skin.

It will probably take around seven to ten days for the wound to heal. During this time, the tip of the penis may be red and raw and there may also be a yellow secretion. It may even become ulcerated if it comes in contact with wet diapers. If there's persistent bleeding, fever, pus-filled blisters, or swelling, consult your pediatrician.

CLEANING YOUR BABY'S BOTTOM

1 **Use the diaper to clear any soiling** If your baby has had a bowel movement, take her diaper off slowly, using the front to remove as much of the mess as possible Fold the diaper over, place in a plastic bag, and put it aside for later disposal.

2 **Wipe the tummy and legs** Holding your baby's legs firmly but gently, clean her tummy area with wet cotton balls. Using fresh cotton balls, clean along her leg folds. Wipe downward and away from the body to avoid transferring any infections to the genital area.

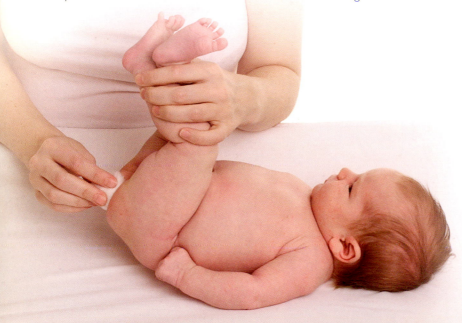

Cleaning a boy

Your baby boy may urinate when you remove his diaper, so do so slowly.

Using fresh cotton balls, wipe his penis using a downward motion—don't pull the foreskin back. Clean around his testicles as well. Holding your baby's ankles, lift his bottom gently and clean his anal area and the backs of his thighs. Pat the whole area thoroughly dry.

3 **Clean a girl's genitals** Hold her ankles gently with one hand, and lift her bottom slightly. Using fresh cotton balls, clean the outer lips of her vulva. Always wipe downward so that you don't transfer bacteria from her anus to her vagina. Then, keeping her bottom raised, clean her buttocks using fresh cotton balls. Clean the backs of her thighs and up her back, if necessary. Dry the area thoroughly.

PREPARING YOUR BABY'S BATH

Some parents like to bathe their baby daily, but there is no real reason to do so. Other than dirty diapers, the only reason a baby gets dirty is if he vomits. A number of babies sweat when they sleep, but this doesn't really cause a baby to become dirty. A bath every two or three days is probably enough. If you would like to make the bath a part of your baby's going-to-bed routine or you simply just want to do it daily, that's fine, too.

Before you start bathing your baby, have everything you need at hand. The first rule of bathing is "never leave your baby unattended in the bath." By being well prepared you won't have to go looking for things holding a wet baby.

If you are using a portable bath, you can wash your baby in any warm, draft-free room. Make sure the bath is well supported on a waterproof surface.

The bath water should be warm but not hot (see page 57).

If you are going to wash your baby's hair, do so before you put her in the bath (see page 58).

Using an adult bath

If you don't have space for a baby bath, or prefer to use the family bath from the start, there are a number of aids to make your baby feel secure and you more confident. The simplest is a foam support cushion that is attached to the bath by suction. You could also sit your baby in a bath ring (which looks like a swimming aid). Both of these can also be used in a baby bath to leave both your hands free to support and wash. From about six months of age, when your baby can sit, a bath "pod" can be used. Some models have a longer seat so that a toddler can join the baby in the bath and play along, too.

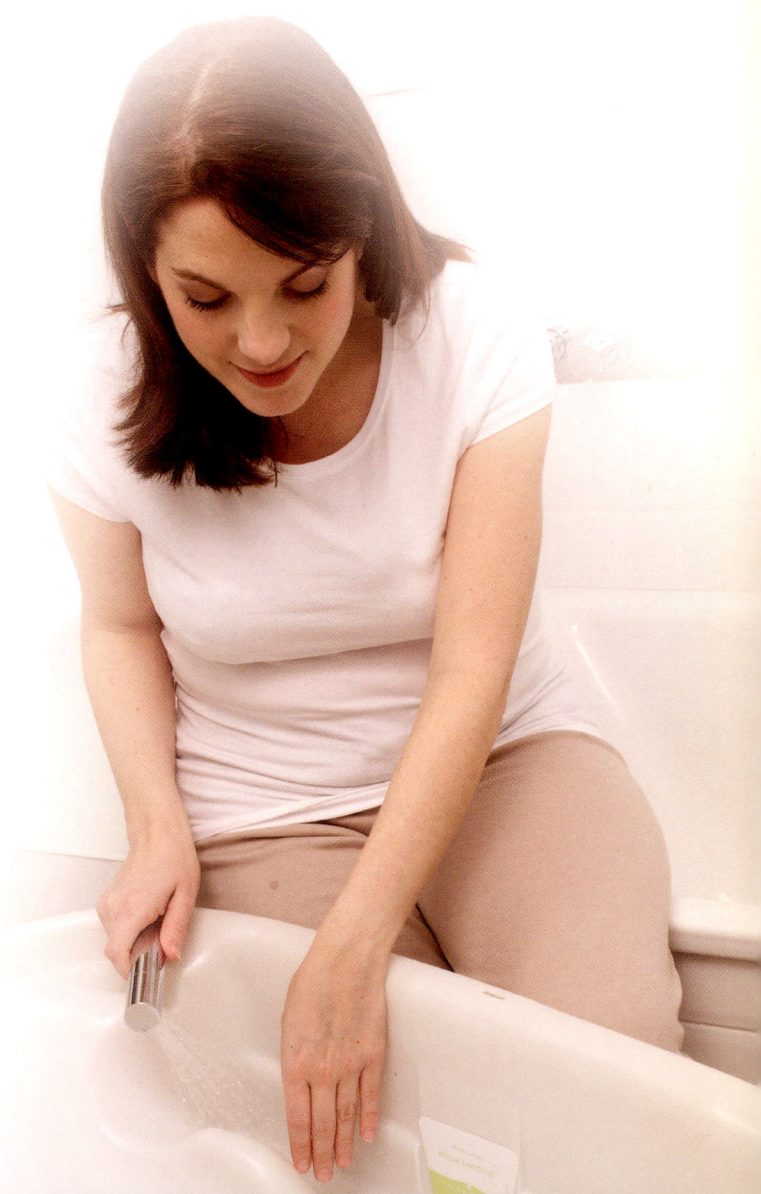

PREPARING TO BATH YOUR BABY

1 **Fill the bath** If your bath does not have a marker, add only 3–4 inches water for babies up to six months old and never more than waist high (in a sitting position) for older babies. Always put cold water in first and then add hot water to make sure there is no risk of your baby being scalded.

2 **Test the temperature** Dip your elbow into the water; it should feel pleasantly warm but not hot. If you are not sure, use a bath thermometer. It should read about 97°F.

Baby bath thermometer

A bath thermometer can give parents peace of mind. Choose a model with an easy-to-read display and long battery life. A warning light when the water is above, say, 102°F is a useful additional feature.

3 **Undress your baby** Sit by the bath with your baby on your lap on her towel. Remove all her clothes then wrap the towel around her to keep her warm. If you are going to wash her hair, do this while she's out of the bath.

WASHING YOUR BABY'S HAIR

You will need to wash your baby's hair and scalp with warm water every couple of days during the first few weeks to remove any sweat and dirt. There is no need for shampoo until your baby's hair has grown, when a gentle baby shampoo can be used. Cradle cap is common on a baby's scalp (see page 67). It is no cause for concern and usually clears up after a few weeks.

Your baby may object quite strongly to having her head wet. Babies especially dislike getting water on their faces or in their eyes, so you should take care to avoid this. There are also special pouring jugs that will direct the water away from her face.

If your baby really hates having her hair washed, or if you are worried about washing your baby's hair, don't force it. You don't have to undress her or put her in a bath. Simply sit her on your lap and wash her hair and head with a damp sponge or washcloth. Pat dry with a soft towel and gently brush her hair. After a couple of weeks, try again.

Remember: your baby will not be happy if she feels insecure, so if she objects to being held under your arm, sit on the edge of the bath and hold her in your lap. Gently pat your baby's head dry.

Hair shield
Many babies dislike shampoo and soapy water getting in their eyes. Modern hair and eye shields are made from foam and fit snugly around the head, with a hole in the top so you can wash the hair.

The fontanelles

When your baby is born, the bones of her skull will not be entirely fused together, leaving small soft patches on the top of her head. These are known as the fontanelles. While you should obviously be careful around these, since they are spots where your baby's brain is vulnerable, they are covered with a tough membrane, so you don't have to avoid them altogether. Simply wash and dry over them gently, as you would the rest of your baby's skin. They won't knit together entirely until she is about two years old.

WASHING YOUR BABY'S HAIR

2 Wet her hair with bath water With your baby tucked under your arm, check the water temperature and, using your free hand, apply some of the water to her hair. If you like, use some specially formulated baby shampoo, then rinse it off.

1 Start by cleaning your baby's face Using cotton balls and cooled boiled water for a young baby (under three months), clean around her eyes and mouth. For an older baby, you can use a washcloth and plain water.

3 Towel-dry her hair Gently pat, rather than rub, your baby's hair dry with a soft towel. Use a corner of the towel as covering her face with the towel may frighten her. Gently brush her hair with a soft-bristled brush.

BATHING YOUR BABY

Until your baby can sit up unsupported—at around six months of age—you will need to support his back and shoulders with one hand all the time he is in the bath. Above all, never leave your baby unattended.

Help your baby enjoy his bath by smiling and talking to him throughout; be gentle and avoid getting water on his face. Take care to ensure that the bath water remains warm.

In general, wash the cleanest parts of your baby first and the dirtiest parts last. This way you cut down on the risk of transferring infection from one part of his body to another.

Bath toys and books

When your baby is older, he will enjoy some simple waterproof toys and books. The best ones are brightly colored and easily graspable.

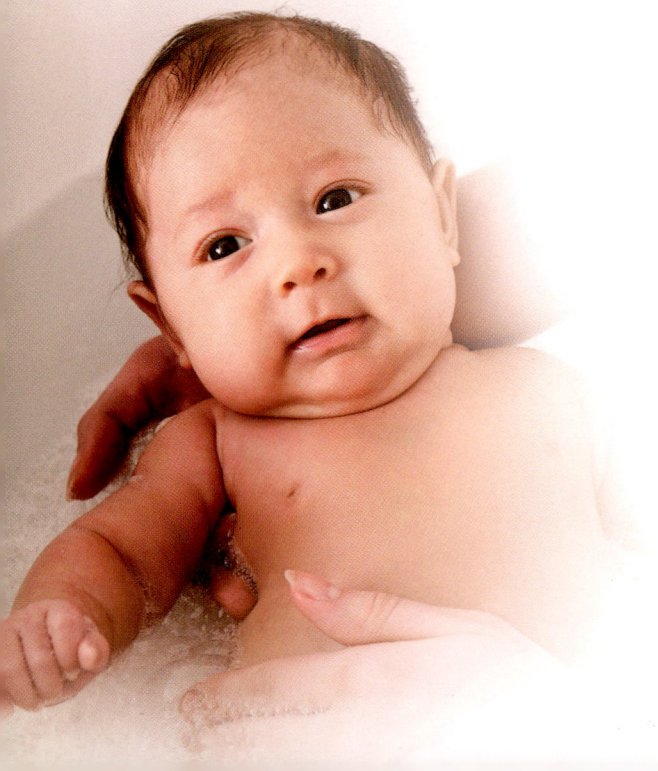

Wet, warm, and relaxed
A baby's bathtime should be full of precious moments so make sure you both enjoy them to the full.

GIVING YOUR BABY A BATH

1 Lower your baby into the bath Unwrap your baby and cradle him in your arms, supporting his bottom half with one hand and his shoulders and head with the other. Lower him into the bath, bottom first.

2 Rinse his torso Still supporting your baby behind his head and shoulders, gently splash water on to his chest and tummy. Smile, chat, and laugh to keep him amused. and feeling secure.

3 Wash his upper back and neck Sit your baby up, holding him under the armpit and supporting his chest across your arm. Rinse his upper back and the back of his neck.

4 Rinse his bottom Still supporting your baby across his chest, tip him forward, keeping his face clear of the water, and using his knees for extra support. Rinse his lower back and bottom.

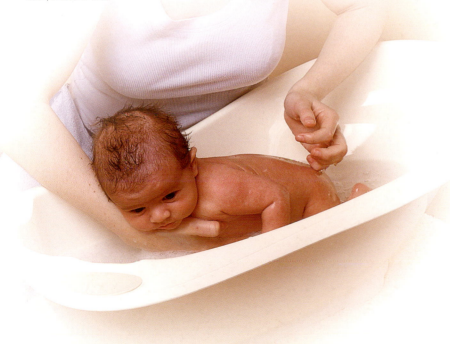

Getting your baby out of the bath

Tip him back on to his bottom. Supporting his head and shoulders, hold him under the armpit and slide your other hand under his bottom. Then, lift him out of the bath.

DRYING YOUR BABY

Have a soft, warmed towel ready to wrap your baby in. Hooded cotton towels are specially made for babies and are snug and cozy. You don't have to use a special one but it is a good idea to reserve some towels for your baby's exclusive use.

As soon as you have removed your baby from the water, wrap him in the towel and cuddle him dry; you should gently pat your baby not rub him. After a warm bath your baby will probably be at his most relaxed, so talk and sing to him and see if he'll respond. This is a great opportunity to make your baby feel loved and secure.

Before you dress him, make sure that all his skin creases, particularly those in the thigh and diaper area, are dry. Any moisture left is likely to cause soreness and irritation.

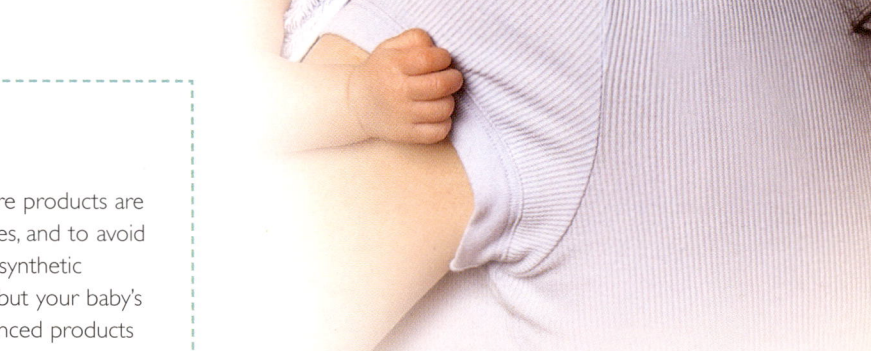

Baby skin care

The simple rules when buying baby skincare products are to choose those specifically made for babies, and to avoid fragranced products and those containing synthetic chemicals. Many products smell gorgeous, but your baby's skin is extremely delicate and highly fragranced products may upset the balance of its natural oils.

DRYING YOUR BABY

1 **Place your baby in the center of the towel** As soon as you take him out of the bath, wrap your baby in a warm towel. Gently fold one side over him but take care not to cover his face, as this may cause him to panic and start crying.

2 **Pat him dry all over** Fold both sides over so that he is completely wrapped up, and gently pat him dry. Pay particular attention to the skin creases around his legs, his diaper area, under his arms, and around his neck.

3 **Keep your baby covered while you dress him** Begin to put on his clothes, keeping the rest of his body covered with the towel. This will help prevent him getting chilled. It's a good idea to use a fresh, clean towel for each bath.

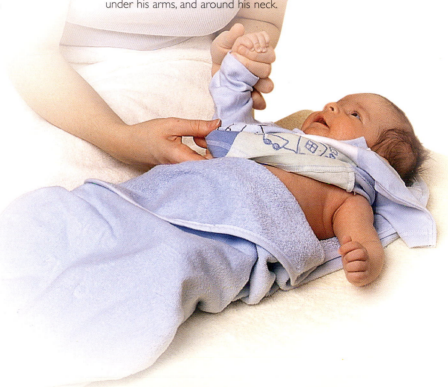

DAILY ROUTINES

In addition to changing and keeping your baby clean, you will have to attend to your newborn's umbilical cord stump until it has dropped off and the site has healed. Your young baby has very sharp nails that should be kept short to prevent her scratching herself, and she may suffer from cradle cap, which will need attention. Once your baby's teeth start to come through, you'll want to begin tooth and gum care. Finally, you will need to know what to do to put her to bed safely.

TAKING CARE OF YOUR BABY'S CORD STUMP

Shortly after birth, the cord is clamped and cut a few inches from your baby's navel. There are no nerves in this area, so this is not a painful procedure for your baby. The cord will gradually shrivel up, turn black, and, within about 10 days, fall off. Some parents, for sentimental or superstitious reasons, choose to keep the remnants of their baby's umbilical cord. Before the cord falls off, however, the navel area is susceptible to infection, particularly if it gets wet or dirty.

TAKE CARE

While a slight discharge after the cord has withered is normal, if the stump exudes pus or blood, or the area around its base becomes inflamed, call your pediatrician. These symptoms may indicate an infection.

Umbilical hernia

You may notice that your baby's navel protrudes when she cries. This swelling is called an umbilical hernia and it is very common in young babies, with one in 10 babies affected.

Newborn babies have an opening in the abdominal wall through which blood vessels extend to the umbilical cord. After the cord is cut, stomach muscles grow and encircle the navel, but sometimes this is not complete. When your baby cries she puts pressure on these weak abdominal muscles, causing the intestines to push through to beneath the surface of her navel. The resulting bulge varies from very small to the size of a golf ball. Surgery is not usually necessary as the opening generally closes up by itself after a year or two.

TAKING CARE OF YOUR BABY'S CORD STUMP

1 **Clean around the stump** Your pediatrician will advise you on what to use to clean your baby's cord stump. Generally, you should use clean cotton balls moistened in cooled, boiled water to gently wipe the stump, the area around it, and the crevices of the navel. After wiping, dry the area gently with another cotton ball.

2 **Expose the stump to the air** The stump will dry and heal much faster if you expose it to air as much as possible. If it does get wet, make sure it is thoroughly dried. When you put on a clean diaper, fold the front down below the stump so the stump is left uncovered. If you're using plastic pants or a wrap, make sure these also don't cover the stump.

3 **After the stump has fallen off** There may be a few spots of blood, and the wound will continue to heal. You should clean and dry it thoroughly daily until the area is completely healed.

CARING FOR YOUR BABY'S HAIR AND NAILS

A good time to see to your baby's hair and nails is after he has had a bath.

Baby hair

Some babies are born with a full head of hair, some have only a sparse covering. Thick or thin, newborn hair is invariably shed after a couple of weeks—often a cause of concern for parents, but perfectly normal. Your baby may also have a covering of downy body hair, known as lanugo. This, too, will rub off within a couple of weeks.

Your baby's hair will need only simple care at first; his young head is particularly sensitive due to the soft areas known as the fontanelles (see page 58). Don't be afraid of handling your baby's head though; simply ensure that any contact with it is carried out with care. Always use a soft brush on your baby's hair. Gentle washing and brushing of your baby's hair should guard against cradle cap (greasy or yellowish scales on the scalp).

Baby nails

A newborn's nails are often quite long and you should trim them to stop him scratching himself or you. Toenails tend to grow more slowly than fingernails but often excess skin encroaches on to the nail bed, making toenails difficult to trim. Use an emery board as, until he is older, cutting with scissors can risk tearing the skin, which is not only uncomfortable for your baby but could also lead to infection.

Trim finger- and toenails after a bath, when they are at their softest, and cut them straight across, leaving no ragged edges. With a young baby, you can gently nibble his nails; your mouth is more sensitive than an emery board or scissors.

Baby mittens

A newborn's nails are very sharp so to prevent your baby scratching himself or irritating any dry skin condition he may have, cover them with a pair of soft, cotton mittens, often called "scratch mittens."

TAKE CARE

Severe or persistent cases of cradle cap may be due to a skin condition such as eczema, which will need professional treatment.

CARING FOR YOUR BABY'S HAIR AND NAILS

Brushing your baby's hair

After wiping your baby's hair down with a damp cloth or sponge or washing it (see page 59), gently brush with a soft-bristled brush. Don't use a comb as this could catch on—and scratch—your baby's scalp.

Treating cradle cap

Gently massage warmed baby oil or aqueous cream into your baby's scalp, leave overnight and, using a soft brush, brush off the scales the following morning. Never pick off the scales as you could cause an infection.

Trimming your baby's nails

Sit your baby comfortably in your lap and hold him securely. Use one hand to steady his fingers and the other to gently file along the natural nail line with an emery board. Go slowly and be as gentle as possible. Special baby nail scissors are also available to trim nails.

File toenails straight across to avoid catching his skin. If you do draw some blood, blot with a tissue then dab some antiseptic ointment on to the area.

CARING FOR YOUR BABY'S TEETH

Once your baby starts teething it is a good idea to get into a daily routine of tooth and gum care, brushing in the morning and last thing at night. If your baby has just one or two teeth, you can use a cloth or some gauze to get rid of the plaque, bacteria, and acid that can cause tooth decay. When your baby has more than a couple of teeth, you should start using a baby toothbrush.

Your baby will not be able to clean her teeth properly for a few years yet, so you will have to take responsibility for this. Your baby will enjoy imitating you, however, so let her have her own brush to play with while she watches you brush your teeth.

Baby toothbrush
Choose a brightly colored toothbrush with soft, rounded bristles. Change it every six to eight weeks, even if it doesn't look worn, because bacteria from your baby's mouth will accumulate on the bristles.

Baby toothpaste
Use specially formulated baby toothpastes, which contain low levels of fluoride. Avoid those that contain added sugar to make them more palatable—this will only encourage plaque. The general rule is to use only a small smear of toothpaste for babies and toddlers.

Limit sugary foods and drinks
Never put your baby to bed with a bottle or let her suck endlessly on a bottle filled with milk or juice, as her teeth will be bathed in sugary fluid, which will encourage tooth decay. On the other hand, give her plenty of raw fruit and vegetables, which are naturally sweet and good to gnaw on.

Check your baby's teeth frequently, and if you see any white, yellow, or brown spots on the teeth, contact your dentist.

Fluoride

Fluoride is a mineral that can help to prevent tooth decay. There are a number of sources of fluoride including toothpaste and tap water. Your pediatrician or dentist can offer advice on suitable levels of fluoride; too much can stain teeth.

Tooth-safe toys
Hard, sharp toys can damage a baby's teeth and gums. For this reason, only let your baby chew on suitably soft but firm objects.

TOOTH CARE

Cleaning one or two baby teeth
Gently wipe your baby's teeth and gums with a clean handkerchief or small piece of gauze to which you have added a tiny amount of baby toothpaste. You can also use cotton buds, if you prefer.

Brushing your baby's teeth
Sit your baby on your lap with her back against you and carefully brush her teeth and gums using a small dab of suitable toothpaste and a soft-bristled toothbrush. A gentle up and down motion will get rid of any plaque. Be careful when brushing the back of her mouth as your child might be frightened of gagging. If you can, discourage your baby from swallowing toothpaste: by encouraging her to spit it out.

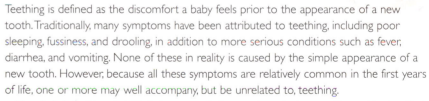

Teething

Teething is defined as the discomfort a baby feels prior to the appearance of a new tooth. Traditionally, many symptoms have been attributed to teething, including poor sleeping, fussiness, and drooling, in addition to more serious conditions such as fever, diarrhea, and vomiting. None of these in reality is caused by the simple appearance of a new tooth. However, because all these symptoms are relatively common in the first years of life, one or more may well accompany, but be unrelated to, teething.

Your baby's first tooth is likely to appear between six and nine months and by her first birthday, she will probably have two to four teeth. She will have her full complement of 20 baby teeth by the age of about three. If your baby does suffer from teething pain, offer a cold hard object to chomp on, such as a teething ring which can be chilled in the freezer. If your baby seems very distressed then baby acetaminophin or a topical analgesic are the best remedies.

PUTTING YOUR BABY TO BED

Your baby will spend a lot of time asleep so it's important that you take steps to protect her while she does so. You need to ensure her bed is a safe, secure place to be, and that you follow the recommendations for minimizing the risk of SIDS (right).

For at least the first six months, have your baby sleep in your bedroom next to your bed. Whether you breast- or bottlefeed, this makes it easy for you to put your baby back in her crib after night feeds. If your baby was premature (before 37 weeks) and/or had a low birth weight (less than 6 lbs), it is much safer for her to sleep in her own crib for the first few months.

Your baby can sleep outside during the day without problems; just make sure that she is protected from drafts, biting insects, and direct sunlight. Indoors or out, you may want to use a listening device to check on her if you are not close by.

In the early weeks, you may wish to put your baby to sleep in something smaller and cosier than a crib, perhaps a Moses basket, bassinet, or a carrycot—a newborn can look small and lonely a regular crib. A basket or carrycot is also portable, meaning your baby can feel at home wherever she sleeps.

TAKE CARE

Also known as crib death, SIDS is every parent's nightmare. Thanks to a number of recent studies, a good deal is now known about how to reduce the risk factors that predispose babies to crib death.

Most important is your baby's sleeping position. You should always put your baby down to sleep on her back, with her feet touching the foot of her crib or Moses basket.

Another important risk factor is smoking—both during and after pregnancy. Exposure to smoke doubles the risk of a baby dying of SIDS. Don't let anyone smoke in the same room as your baby and don't burn incense in her room.

SIDS is more common in winter, probably as a result of babies becoming overheated. Keep the room temperature at 61–68°F and use several light blankets instead of one heavy cover. Don't use pillows or crib bumpers, which can prevent air circulating and lead to a build-up of heat.

PUTTING YOUR BABY TO BED

1 **Check the suitability of her bed** Make sure your baby's basket, crib, or carrycot is free of bumpers, pillows, sheepskins and quilts.

2 **Dress her and the bed appropriately** Your baby should be lightly clothed for sleep – generally an undershirt, diaper, and sleepsuit is fine; do not overdress her. Make sure her head is not covered. Use light, cotton bedding and blankets (or an appropriate baby sleep bag). Always put your baby down on her back.

3 **Feet to foot** By placing your baby with her feet to the foot of her bed, you prevent her from wriggling down under the covers. This way she can move as she wants to without the risk of getting the covers over her head.

Baby sleeping bag

If your baby is active, you may feel happier dressing her in a sleep bag, which cannot be thrown off. You need to choose one based on your baby's weight rather than age. If the bag is too big, there is a risk of her slipping down inside. Sleeping bags usually have a tog measurement, or warmth rating; the higher the tog, the warmer the bag. A 2.5 tog bag is recommended for standard conditions.

GETTING CLOSER TO YOUR BABY

Your young baby will not need much amusement but he will benefit from intimate activities with you. Touch is a primary means of communication, so he will appreciate being stroked and massaged. As he gets older, he will enjoy being read to as well as engaging in other activities with you. All these help to cement the parent-child bond and give you more confidence in handling your baby.

GENTLE TOUCHING

Sensory exchange in the form of touching is vital to the well-being of both parents and their babies. For that reason, mothers and babies are no longer physically separated in the early hours and days after birth unless there is a medical reason to do so. It is therefore important that both parents communicate their strong feelings for their baby through close physical contact. It's ideal if, during a baby's initial alert period after the birth, you hold him naked against your skin so that he becomes familiar with how you feel and smell. You should continue this when you get home and also talk to him in a quiet soothing voice. As he gets older, your baby will try to copy the noises you make to him and will want to imitate your facial expressions.

Through bonding in this way, your baby will begin to get to know you, learn to rely on you, and trust you. Make sure your partner has plenty of contact with baby, too, so that your baby can develop an attachment to both of you.

Most very young babies feel vulnerable when they are naked, but will respond well to gentle, non-intrusive stroking—first through clothes and at the right time in the right environment, when naked (see pages 74–75).

Bonding and attachment

These two words are often used interchangeably, although they mean different things. Bonding has more to do with parents relating to their baby, while attachment focuses on how a baby relates to his primary carer (most often his mother).

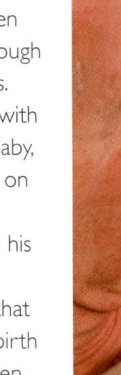

Initially, it was thought that there was a crucial post-birth time for bonding to happen, and that if it didn't happen then, it was somehow too late. Now it is recognized that attachment and bonding are processes, not events; they can certainly start at birth (or even before) but they continue to develop over time.

GENTLE TOUCHES

1 **Relax his limbs** Sit with your baby on your lap. Lower the hand under his bottom to encourage him to straighten his legs. With your other hand, massage his tummy from side to side.

2 **Stroke his shoulders and arms** Now bring your hands over his shoulders and squeeze softly with relaxed open hands. Go on to stroke gently down the length of his arms.

3 **Massage his head, neck, and back** Sit your baby sideways on your thigh so that he leans forward with his arms extended over your forearm. With relaxed, open hands, gently stroke from your baby's head to the base of his spine and up again.

4 **Rock him on your knees** Gently lay him with his tummy forward over your thigh with his legs supported between yours. Gently rock your baby while rubbing the sides of his upper back and arms to relax his arms and shoulders.

5 **Pat him rhythmically** When he is happy and relaxed, straighten his legs over your thighs while continuing to rock gently. Pat, rub, and rock him gently as you stroke down the length of his back and legs,

BABY MASSAGE

From about six to eight weeks of age, your baby will settle into a quiet state of wakefulness, and this is a good time to introduce bare skin massage. Once your baby is happy to be rubbed, rocked, and stroked naked, the skin-to-skin touches will help your baby to feel even more content and further promote the feelings of closeness between you two. Massage also aids digestion, relaxes the tummy, and encourages feelings of tranquillity.

Create a welcoming environment; make the room warm and quiet and lay your baby on a warm, soft, doubled bath towel. Talk to her softly as you slowly remove her clothes. Take off any jewelry that could scratch your baby's skin and make sure your hands are clean and warmed—rub them together and give them a shake to loosen them up before you lay hands on your baby. Keep your movements relaxed and rhythmic.

As time goes on, your baby's periods of wakefulness will become longer, so you will have more opportunities for massage. Getting your baby used to being touched and stroked at an early age will help to make a more formal massage routine easier and more enjoyable for you both later on.

The dad factor

Practicing massage strokes helps a father develop his touch, fosters trust, increases the dad's confidence in his ability to change and bath his baby, and to help more with the daily responsibilities of childcare. Massage will also help to strengthen the physical and emotional relationship between father and baby. By learning how to handle his baby better, a father is more able to soothe and comfort his baby at times when the baby's mother needs to take a break.

Establish eye contact
Look at your baby while you are massaging, keeping eye contact the whole time to make her feel secure and loved.

BABY MASSAGE

1 **Stroke from the neck to the base of the spine** Lay down on your left side, with your baby facing you, lying on her right side. Stroke your baby with the whole of your right hand—from the back of her neck to the base of her spine—for about a minute.

2 **Gently massage your baby's back** Using circular movements, work along the top of her back and then right down its length to the base of her spine. Continue for another minute.

3 **Stroke down the arms** Next, keeping your touch gentle and relaxed, stroke from her shoulder, along her arm to her hand. Do this for about a minute.

4 **End with the legs** Stroke down from her hip to her foot with your palm. Give her leg a little gentle shake to loosen it up and help her relax. Continue for about a minute then roll her gently on to her left side and repeat steps 3 and 4 with her other arm and leg.

READING TO YOUR BABY

Reading is a great bonding experience for parents and their children: there's a special closeness that comes from sharing a story. For parents, time spent reading together ensures they connect with their child and shut out the world. Making sure you set time aside for reading is one way that you and your baby can relax together. Treat it as a special time, a luxury that you can enjoy, and a way of sharing your love.

Very early on, your baby will not understand what you are saying, nor will she appreciate any pictures, but she will soon start to identify words and sentiments through the tone of your voice. Watching the range of expressions on your face gives your baby valuable insights into the plot, and helps her recognize language. Therefore, the way you use your voice, its tone and pace, can make a huge difference to her understanding.

As your child develops, she will gain more from each reading session. Slowly her attention span will increase and she will be able to reach out and touch a book, and make sense of the pictures.

Choosing books

Buy three or four picture books and alternate between them so you don't get bored. Pick tales that you enjoy as you'll be reading them over and over. You need to retain your enthusiasm for the tales, as your baby will notice the pitch and tone of your voice and respond accordingly—and soon start to notice if you skip bits. Go for stories with interesting characters that allow you to use different tones of voice and facial expressions.

Stories with repetitive key words and sounds are a great way to hold your baby's interest, and rhyming tales work well with slightly older children who are fascinated by the ebb and flow of the rhyme and its pattern.

Reading toy

A doll, teddy, or other animal can be used as a helpful character to reinforce your baby's sense of security. If you introduce one at an early age, it will become a part of your baby's process of learning about the world. She will come to associate a favorite cuddly toy with reading time and colorful books and stories, and it will inspire a sense of comfort and expectation in the proceedings.

READING TO YOUR BABY

Start as early as you like

Soon after birth your baby will recognize your voice, so reading will be a soothing experience. It's never too soon to pick up a book and share it with your baby. It can also be a fulfilling—and effective—way to calm a crying baby.

Pick appropriate books

The bright and colorful images in picture books will appeal to babies as will pop-up books and those with tactile pages; all add to the reading experience.

Engage your baby's attention

Use a lot of repetition, saying phrases over again and going through each section slowly. If your baby shows interest by pointing, gazing at the pictures, or making noises, go through it again.

Let your baby enjoy the experience

If your baby wants to reach out, touch, or even chew the book, then let her. She is still paying attention to you, and familiarizing herself with the book at the same time.

BABY WORKOUTS

Playing with your baby will not only be enjoyable but can help promote his physical development and coordination. It's important to provide your baby with opportunities for trying out new movements safely. Offer enthusiastic encouragement every time he achieves a new position, with or without your help, as this will make these activities more enjoyable for your baby.

A good time to start these games is when your baby is about three months old; he'll be more alert and will begin to follow you with his eyes and ears. At this age, too, his muscles will be growing stronger and he'll be able to hold up his head for longer.

Mom and baby exercise

As well as playing physical games with your baby, there's no reason why your baby can't join in as you do a physical workout. Babies make ideal "weights"or, at the very least, will happily lie alongside while you do your push-ups, squats, or whatever.

Encourage your older baby to move

Use attention-grabbing objects that either make an interesting noise or are decorated with high-contrast patterns or colors and place them just out of reach so that your baby has to move to get to them. Later on, you can encourage movement by spacing cushions, stools, or chairs at different intervals around the room to create crawl or cruise spaces.

Swiping
Gradually your baby's involuntary and uncoordinated movements will take on a new purpose—particularly if you hold things just out of reach.

BABY WORKOUTS

Encourage your baby to raise his head

Try placing a rolled-up towel under your baby's chest when he's awake and lying on his front. He will need this support for his head and neck until his muscles are strong enough for him to raise his head on his own.

Strengthen your baby's arm and neck muscles

When he is lying on his back, take your baby's hands and pull him slightly, but let him help to lift his head and neck. This will encourage him progressively to take control of the movement himself.

Exercise your baby's knee and thigh muscles

Flex his legs and let him press the soles of his feet against the palms of your hand. This also benefits the pelvic area.

Encourage your baby's grasp

First make eye contact by shaking a rattle just above his head then move the toy from side to side at chest level.

BABY PLAY

Your baby's play reflects her stage of mental, physical, and sensory development. At first she will enjoy looking at moving objects and brightly colored toys. By two months of age, as her coordination improves, she may begin swiping at things, particularly hanging mobiles. By three months, your baby will be hitting and touching objects to get the feel of them so she needs eye-catching objects that will stay within her reach. By five months, she will want to put everything in her mouth, so choose your toys carefully—small and light enough for her to manipulate, but chunky enough to prevent choking.

Bear in mind that your baby has a very short attention span. Don't waste money on expensive toys that she will quickly lose interest in—simple household objects such as keys or an empty box will do just as well. Also, remember that you are the most stimulating and responsive plaything your baby could want. Through simple play you can help your baby develop healthy emotional, physical, and intellectual skills.

When you do buy toys, choose brightly colored ones that make noises; these will more easily capture a young baby's interest. Interactive toys with moving parts, levers and buttons, will help her dexterity and teach her about cause and effect.

Recommended toys

Age	Toys
2–4 months	Rattles; mobiles; brightly colored board books
4–7 months	Textured toys that make sounds; baby mirror; baby books with board, cloth, or vinyl pages
8–12 months	Stacking, push-pull, and bath toys; large building blocks; "busy boxes" that open, close, and squeak

First games
Even a month-old baby will enjoy trying to imitate your gestures; try sticking out your tongue, opening and closing your mouth widely or smiling.

BABY PLAY

A basketful of toys
Babies have short attention spans so a large number of simple toys, rather than a few expensive ones, are preferable. Babies also enjoy putting objects into and taking them out of containers.

Stacking toys
Large, easily graspable rings and blocks can be enjoyed on their own as well as being arranged on supports or on top of each other.

Rattles
Brightly colored, textured toys that contain integral bells or beads and can be easily grasped and brought to the mouth will amuse your baby. Make sure toys are machine washable!

Mirrors
From six weeks on, your baby will enjoy looking in the mirror with you, seeing the expressions on your faces. As she grows older, however, she will become more interested in her own reflection and will be able to point to things she finds interesting.

Soft toys
Teddies, dolls, and other stuffed animals in soft fabrics are very comforting for babies, though for safety's sake, toys should be removed from the crib once she's asleep.

SENSORY EXPERIENCES

Whether you are indoors or out and about (see page 86), it's a good idea to give your baby a wide range of experiences. As well as offering him different toys and different places to see, you should hold, carry, or place him in varying positions—across your lap on his stomach, on the floor on his back, lying on one side in his crib, or propped upright against your shoulder—throughout the day. Lifting your baby up into the air above your head will also give him thrilling new sensations of movement and gravity, as well as a view of the world from a high vantage point.

Whenever you let your baby "experiment" with new sensations, make sure you keep an eye on him and never give him anything that could put him in danger.

SENSORY EXPERIENCES

Fascinate your baby with feathers
Use a soft and colorful plume to stroke your baby from top to bottom and place it between his toes and fingers. Let him experiment with holding it himself.

Amuse him with squelchy sacks
Fill some heavy-duty freezer bags with different volumes of water and add a few drops of a different food coloring to each. Secure tightly. Use cool water for some, warm water for others. Your baby can feel a bag's weight in one hand and perhaps transfer it to the other. Put the bag on different parts of his body to introduce him to different sensations.

Catch his eye with color
Colorful moving objects are very intriguing to young babies. It's easy to make a portable mobile that can be moved close to his field of vision so he can reach out and play. Tie some colorful ribbons to the fingertips of a glove and move it across his field of vision, letting him grasp it if he chooses.

Fill his ears with happy noises
Add bells, beads, or buttons to a pair of your baby's socks. Lay your baby face up and place the socks on his feet. If necessary, lift his bottom and move his feet to get his attention. Do not leave him alone with the socks!

DEVELOPMENTAL MILESTONES

The recognized stages of a baby's development are generally termed "milestones." All babies differ, but most will reach developmental milestones at around the same age, and in a predictable order.

There are two kinds of physical milestones. "Gross" skills are related to movement, so holding the head up, as well as rolling, crawling, and walking are gross motor skills. "Fine" skills are those movements he makes with his hands and fingers, such as grasping, pointing, and gripping. In addition to these physical milestones, there are measurable mental, sensory, social, and emotional milestones which are intimately linked to your baby's physical growth and abilities.

Each area of development supports other areas. Your baby wants to watch a mobile and reach for a rattle or touch your face and play with your hair; he needs to do these things and starts to do them as soon as he has gained the necessary skills to do them.

The chart on page 85 indicates the order in which most babies are likely to acquire various skills, and the approximate age at which they will acquire them.

Every baby is different

The chart on page 85 offers a rough guide only. Babies develop skills at different speeds: some will be quicker than others in acquiring all skills while others may make faster progress with motor skills than social or mental skills.

Cruise control

Your baby will sit before he crawls and may crawl before he stands—though some babies skip crawling altogether. The final stage before he walks unaided is likely to be cruising around the furniture.

The first year's milestones

Month 1
Your baby likes to look at faces and responds to eye contact. He may turn toward a voice he recognizes. He may mimic your facial expressions.

Month 2
Your baby smiles in response to you and his gurglings and cooings have the shape of speech, with gaps, stops, and starts. You can have a "conversation" with him. He likes to be held and rocked.

Month 3
Your baby laughs and giggles with delight and smiles spontaneously when he hears your voice. He may roll over.

Month 4
A moving object will grab your baby's attention and he tries to reach out for something he likes. He delights in being around the people closest to him. He may sit with support.

Month 5
Your baby likes to look at himself in the mirror and enjoys playing "peek-a-boo." He can hold objects in both hands and examine their textures.

Month 6
Your baby can clearly express emotions in his face and voice —joy, displeasure, fear, anticipation, or worry. He puts everything in his mouth to examine it.

Month 7
Your baby understands that something still exists even if he can't see it; this shows he has grasped there is a world outside what he can see, feel, and hear. He babbles and make consonant sounds like "ma-ma." He may start to crawl.

Month 8
A baby can anticipate daily events. So, the sound of a key in the door and it opening means "daddy's home!" He shows pleasure and may imitate sounds.

Month 9
Separation anxiety becomes common and your baby may object strongly when you leave the room. He gets upset if you remove a toy from his hands. He lifts his arms to signal he wants to be picked up.

Month 10
Your baby can understand "No" and may even shake his head as if he knows this means "No." He enjoys "reading" a book with you and knows that if he turns a page, something new will appear. He may stand with help.

Month 11
Your baby starts to pretend play by combing dolly's hair or cuddling a teddy. He understands that playing "having a cup of tea" in the bath is not real and he'll laugh at the game. He may stand unaided.

Month 12
Your baby begins to use his index finger to point and can grasp a small object between his fingers and thumb. He may walk a few steps without help.

GOING PLACES TOGETHER

It's never too soon to include your baby in your outings as long as you take certain precautions. It is a good idea to avoid crowds and rush-hour traffic and transport, where you may be jostled, and exposing your baby to people who may be ill.

There is no special age your baby needs to be before you take her out, as long as you are well prepared and your baby is appropriately dressed. Your baby can't fully regulate her body temperature so dress her in one more layer of clothing than you would wear in the same environment.

A little preparation beforehand—in the form of a well-stocked travel bag—can help make outings highly enjoyable. Choose different places to go, perhaps the park one day and the mall the next; many locations offer mother-and-baby activities.

Don't be put off by weather conditions: it's good for a baby to experience the different effects of climate. She should feel both wind and sun on her face (as long as she is appropriately dressed), and hear the sound of rain on the stroller hood or witness the world transformed by a covering of snow.

Travel bag essentials

- Changing mat with plastic backing; these sometimes come attached to the bag
- Disposable diapers
- Plastic bag or sack for used diapers
- Cotton balls or baby wipes
- Baby lotion
- Bottle of made-up formula or carton of formula and a clean bottle (if you are not breastfeeding)
- Water or juice in a bottle
- Baby food and spoon (for babies over about six months)
- Bib
- Muslin cloth to clean up any dribble
- Rattle or other toy such as a soft book to amuse your baby
- Change of clothes
- Sunscreen and sunhat (in summer)
- Pacifier (optional)

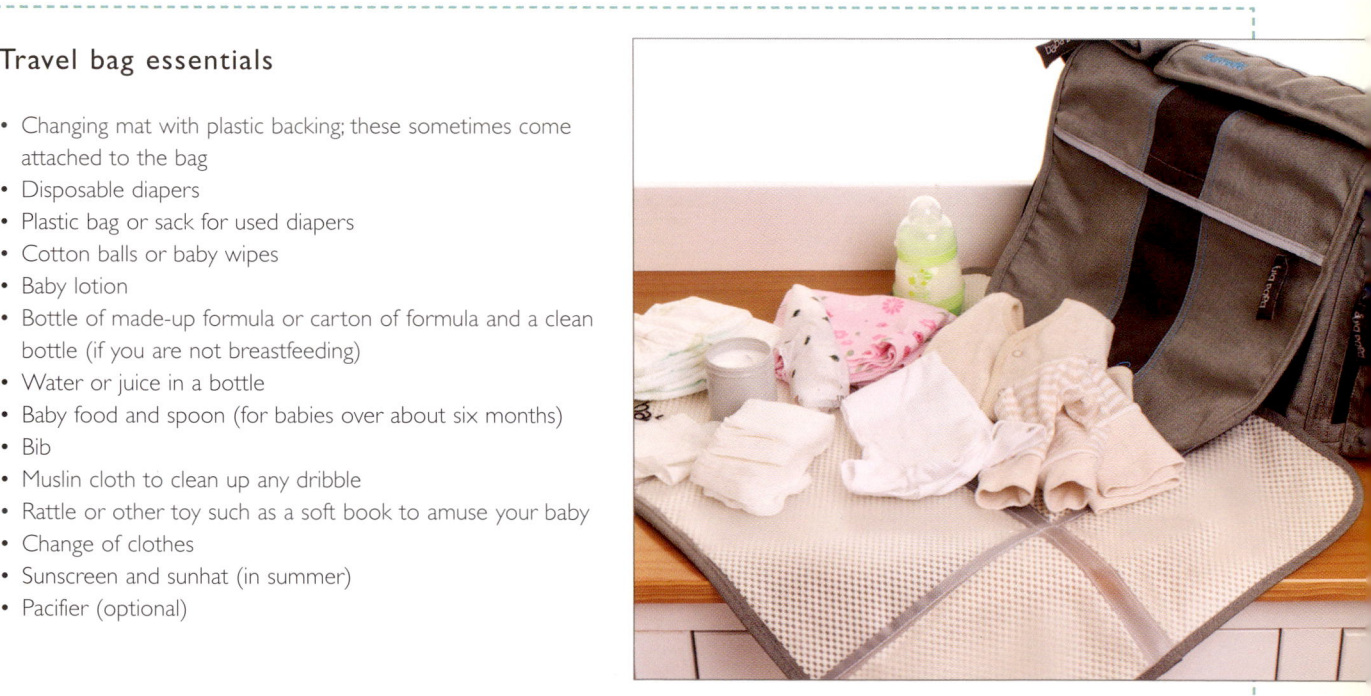

HELPS WHEN GOING OUT AND ABOUT

Dining seats

There are several portable and booster seats to hold a baby safely and comfortably on almost any chair when dining out. Even a baby-friendly restaurant can run out of highchairs! Buy according to your baby's age and weight.

Carriages and strollers

Your choice of baby transport is largely a trade-off between portability and comfort. Your baby will have a smoother ride in a traditional carriage or three- or two-in-one system (in which the same wheeled chassis can be used with a lie-flat carry cot for a newborn and sit-in "chair" as he gets older), but neither of these is particularly useful if you use public transport a lot. If you drive most places, make sure you can collapse and reopen a stroller easily and fit it in the trunk of your car. A rain cover and sunshade are good extras and a net or tray for shopping is also useful.

Slings and carriers

A sling or carrier keeps your baby close to you and can be less hassle than a stroller, especially if you have to use public transport. Buy according to your baby's weight and make sure the straps fit comfortably (see pages 12–15).

Car seats

A car seat is vital from the moment your baby leaves the hospital; make sure you choose one appropriate to your baby's weight and that it is fitted correctly. A baby is safest in a rear-facing seat in the back of the car. Do not fit a baby car seat where there is an air bag.

ILLNESS AND EMERGENCIES

Emergency situations that need an immediate 911 call are: your baby is unconscious or having difficulty breathing; he is having convulsions; he is unusually drowsy or floppy, blue, or very pale; and if your baby has a purple-red rash that does not fade when pressed (see page 89).

Additional signs that merit an immediate call to your pediatrician are listed below although, if something is not listed but you feel it may indicate that your baby is unwell or in pain, don't hesitate to ring your doctor.

IF YOU THINK YOUR BABY IS ILL

New babies can become ill very quickly, so it is important to be aware of the symptoms that could indicate illness (see box, right). If ever you make an office or hospital visit, be prepared to take with you as much information as you can about your baby's condition, such as if and when he exhibited any of the symptoms listed above and right (or any others that worry you). If you have recorded any observations, so much the better.

Keep in mind that a combination of symptoms is more serious than any one appearing in isolation.

A basic check to perform whenever you suspect your baby is sick is to take his temperature. Normal body temperature for a baby is 98,6°F (37°C). When the immune system is fighting infection this will rise, producing a fever, while a serious drop indicates hypothermia. Take the temperature more than once, since it may be fluctuating. The most accurate reading is given by an ear thermometer, though many parents prefer to use the underarm method. The least accurate reading is given by using a strip on the forehead. Make sure you record your readings.

Call your pediatrician immediately if your baby

- Seems more sleepy than normal, especially at times when he is normally alert and active
- Seems more floppy than usual
- Is crying more than usual or has a cry that sounds different from his usual cry
- Is eating or drinking less than usual
- Is passing less urine than usual
- Is vomiting
- Has extended diarrhea (more than 6 hours) or Is passing blood in his stools
- Has a raised (100.4°F [38°C]) or very low (95°F [35°C]} temperature
- Has a severe or persistent cough or one that brings up phlegm when he coughs (a productive cough)
- Seems to be having problems breathing
- Has one or more purplish-red spots (see also page 89)

CHECKING YOUR BABY'S VITAL SIGNS

Taking your baby's pulse

Parents are not normally required to take a baby's pulse except when recommended to do so by a doctor during illness.

The normal pulse rate for a young baby is quite high—between 100 and 160 beats per minute (bpm). A one year old's pulse slows to 100 to 120 bpm. A baby's pulse should be taken on the inside of the upper arm between the elbow and shoulder. Press your index and middle fingers gently against an artery until you can feel a beat. Then count the number of heart beats in 15 seconds and multiply by four to get the bpm.

Taking an underarm temperature

This is the recommended method for everyday use. You can use either a digital or a mercury thermometer. Cradle your baby on your lap. Wipe dry his armpit, shake down the thermometer and put the bulb into the fold of his armpit. Hold his arm flat against his side, and leave for at least five minutes. The underarm is about 0.6°C lower than the internal body temperature.

The normal underarm temperature is 97.5°F (36.4°C).

> ## TAKE CARE
>
> Do not take your baby's temperature orally with a mercury thermometer in case he bites on and breaks the bulb—mercury is highly toxic.

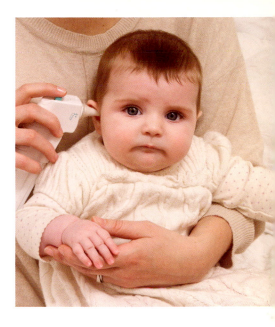

Taking an ear temperature

An ear thermometer works by measuring the temperature of the eardrum and surrounding tissues, to give a highly accurate and instantaneous reading.

Checking a rash for meningitis

Press a glass firmly over any pin-prick red spots or large purple marks to see if they fade or turn white under pressure. If the spots and rash are still visible through the glass, seek urgent medical attention. Whatever the appearance of a rash, you should seek advice immediately if you have any concerns.

CARING FOR AN ILL BABY

After you have consulted your pediatrician and determined the cause of your baby's illness, you will need to follow your doctor's instructions; your main task may be to give your baby prescribed medication and keep her as comfortable as possible.

It may be distressing as a parent to witness your baby in physical discomfort but you can help by providing a warm and caring environment. Ill babies in particular will want to be in very close contact with their mothers and will seek a lot more physical attention. If you are breastfeeding, you may find your baby wanting to suckle simply for comfort.

If your baby has been vomiting, had diarrhea or a high temperature, you need to ensure she takes sufficient fluids to replace those she has lost. A high fever can be dangerous, so you should try and bring her temperature down. Make sure she is not wearing too many clothes, and ensure a good supply of fresh air to her room. Try sponging your baby down with tepid water; this will help her feel less irritable and more comfortable.

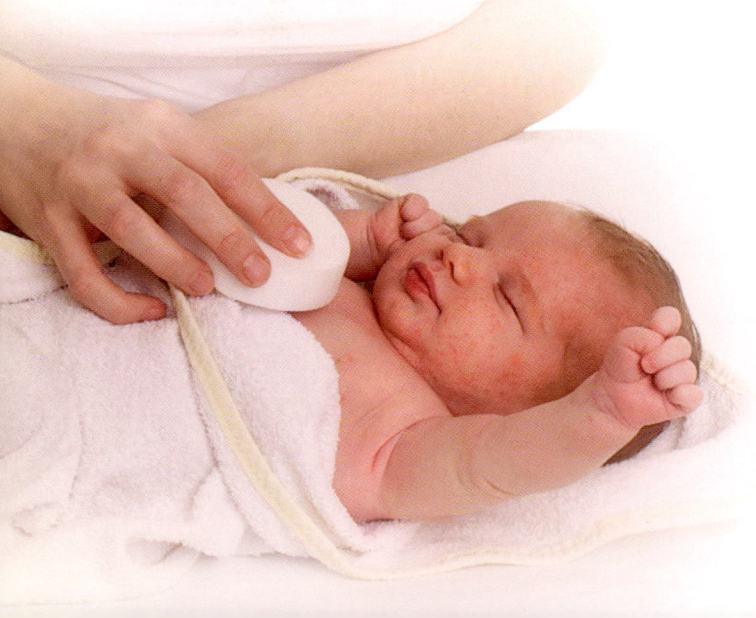

Home care kit

It's a good idea to keep all the following items in one place in the nursery, so that you know exactly where to go when you need them.

Essential items:
Digital thermometer
Nasal aspirator
Medicine dispenser/syringe/droppers
Clean sponge or washcloth
Cotton balls
Favorite toy

Feeding and cleaning items:
Washed bottles
Cartons of ready-to-feed formula
Diapers
Wipes
Bibs or dribble cloths
Towels and washcloths

Daily care items:
Emery boards
Bath thermometer
Baby toothbrush
Soft-bristled hairbrush
Scissors
Tweezers

CARING FOR AN ILL BABY

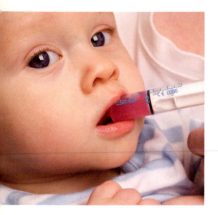

Giving medicine by oral syringe

Cradle your baby in your arms and aim the tip of the syringe between her rear gums and cheek, avoiding the taste buds. Squirt the medicine slowly to avoid making her choke, and do not touch the back of her tongue with the syringe, since this could cause gagging.

Giving medicine by pacifier-style syringe

The nipple-shaped tip of a pacifier-style syringe allows your baby to suck while you express the medicine. Hold your baby in your lap, supporting her head in the crook of your elbow. Put the tip of the syringe in her mouth as you would with a bottle and slowly press the plunger.

Administering ear drops

Lay your baby on her side, with the affected ear uppermost. You need to drop the medicine down the ear canal, so pull back the lobe to straighten the canal, and put the dropper close to her ear. Hold your baby steady while the drops sink in—use cotton balls to soak up any leaks.

Administering eye drops

Swaddle your baby to prevent her from wriggling, and lay her on her back. Tilt her head to one side, with the affected eye nearest your leg. Taking care not to touch the eye with the dropper, pull down her lower eyelid and squeeze the drops between it and the eye. You may need help to hold her head steady.

Sponging

Wrap your baby in a towel and sit her on your lap. Use a damp sponge soaked in boiled water cooled to a tepid temperature to wipe her down. Do not use cold water. As your baby cools, pat her skin dry with the towel, and cover her with a cotton sheet.

FIRST AID FOR BABIES

These instructions are no substitute for proper training in first aid, but they could help to save your baby's life. Always call out for help in an emergency so that someone can contact the emergency services (911) while you attend to your baby. Your priorities are to check that your baby's airway is clear, that he is breathing and that he has a pulse of around 120–160 beats per minutes, depending on his age. If you suspect a spinal injury, do not move your baby and try to ensure that he lies as still as possible.

ELECTRIC SHOCK

A crawling baby may stick his fingers into an unprotected outlet or chew on an electrical cable. A severe electric shock can stop the heart, interfere with breathing, cause shock, convulsions, and severe burns. Your priority is to break the circuit your baby is forming without getting electrocuted yourself.

Call 911 for an ambulance immediately.

Disconnect the plug, if possible, or switch off the circuit breaker. If you can't, stand on some dry non-conductive material such as wood or plastic and push your baby away using a chair leg or broom handle. As a last resort, pull your baby away by his clothes. Check for burns; if present, cover with a sterile dressing or plastic wrap.

If your baby is unconscious (doesn't respond when you call his name or tap the sole of his foot [do not shake him]) place him in the recovery position (page 94). If he is not breathing, you will need to perform rescue breaths and CPR (see page 94).

POISONING

Take extra care to keep hazardous substances out of reach, and make sure that medicines have child-proof caps. For questions about poisoning, call your local poison control center or the American Association of Poison Control Centers at (800)222-1222.

Suspect poisoning if your baby is vomiting, dizzy, having convulsions, or is unconscious, and/or if there are burns or discoloration around the mouth.

Call 911 immediately. Try and discover what he took, how much, and how long ago, so that you can inform the paramedics. Keep a sample of any vomit he produces but don't try and make him sick. You can give him sips of water. If he is unconscious but breathing, put him in the recovery position (page 94).

If your baby is not breathing, check for any obstructions in his mouth and remove it, then give rescue breaths (see page 95).

BLEEDING

Severe blood loss could send your baby into shock (see page 94), and must be dealt with promptly (call 911). Your first objective is to stem the flow of blood. To reduce the risk of cross-infectioin, use disposable gloves, if available.

Lay your baby down and, if an arm or leg is injured, keep the limb raised. Expose the wound by cutting away clothing, if necessary. Check whether something is embedded in the wound. If so, apply pressure on both sides, with a clean dressing but do not press on the foreign body itself. Build up padding around the object before bandaging to avoid putting pressure on it.

If nothing is embedded, press on the wound with your hand, ideally over a clean pad, and secure with a bandage.

If the wound is spurting blood (an artery is cut), apply pressure for at least 10 minutes, then put on a pressure bandage. If blood seeps through, do not replace the dressing but wrap another one around the first dressing.

CHOKING

If your baby is choking but can still cry and cough, check his mouth, being careful not to push any obstruction further down the throat. Use only one finger to fish out the obstruction. Pat his back gently. Only attempt the sequence below if he is conscious but cannot cry, cough (or only weakly), or breathe, or if he is making high-pitched noises.

If you do the following but still cannot feel a pulse, you must call the emergency services (911) and be prepared to perform CPR (see page 95).

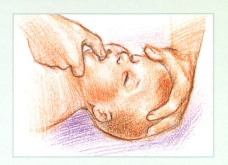

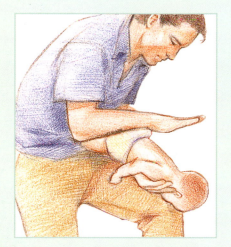

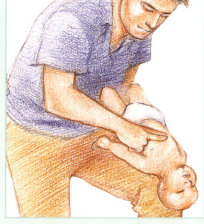

1 **Give five back blows** Lay your baby face down along your forearm with his head low and support his back and chin. Give up to five back blows between his shoulder blades. Check his mouth and very carefully after each blow, using one finger only to remove any obvious obstruction. If the obstruction persists, go to step 2.

2 **Give five chest thrusts** If he still doesn't cry, turn him onto his back and give up to five chest thrusts. Push with two fingertips, inward and upward in the middle of his chest, one finger's breadth below the nipple line, at a rate of one thrust every three seconds. Once again, check the mouth and remove any obvious obstructions after each thrust. If the obstruction does not clear after three cycles of back blows and chest thrusts, call 911. Continue cycles of back blows and chest thrusts until help arrives, and resuscitate (see page 95, if necessary.)

3 **If your baby becomes unconsciousness** Place him on to a firm surface and open his airway, by placing one hand on his forehead and tilting it back slightly and lifting his chin with one finger. Without feeling blindly down the throat, carefully remove any obvious obstruction from the mouth. Check your baby's breathing for up to 10 seconds by listening for sounds of breathing, feeling for breath on your cheek, and looking along his chest for signs of movement.

4 **If your baby remains unconscious and stops breathing** If another person is present, get him or her to call 911 immediately. Give two effective rescue breaths (see page 95) by sealing your lips tightly around your baby's mouth and nose and breathing into his lungs until his chest rises. If his chest doesn't rise, perform CPR (see page 95) for one minute then call call 911. Continue with CPR until your baby moves or help arrives.

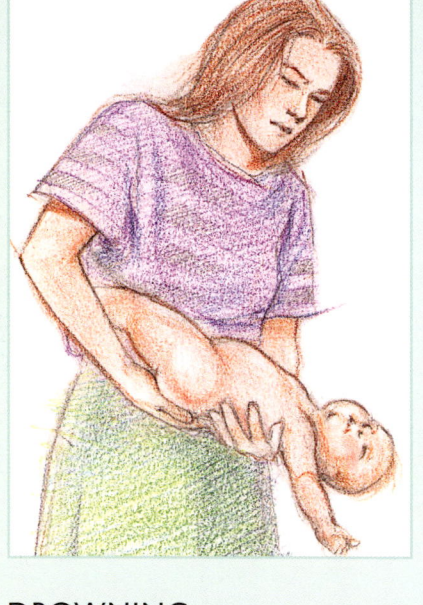

SHOCK

Shock is life threatening; it occurs when organs such as the heart and brain are deprived of oxygen. Warning signs include cold, clammy skin; pallor and a grayish tinge around the lips and nails; fast, shallow breathing; yawning or sighing; and (in extreme cases) loss of consciousness.

Dial 911 immediately. Lay your baby on a coat or blanket, turn her head to the side, in case she vomits, and raise her feet above the level of her heart. Loosen any clothing and keep her warm, but not hot. Check her breathing and pulse frequently. If breathing stops, perform rescue breathing and CPR, (see page 95) if necessary.

DROWNING

A baby who slips under the water in a bath—no matter how shallow—may drown in a couple of minutes if water covers her mouth and nose.

If you find your baby in water, lift her out immediately and hold her so that her head is lower than her body. This will help prevent water or vomit, getting into her lungs. If she is unconscious but still breathing, hold her in the recovery position while you call the emergency services (911). If she is not breathing you must give rescue breaths and CPR, if necessary (see page 95). Water in the lungs will mean you will have to breathe more firmly than usual to get the lungs inflated.

UNCONSCIOUSNESS

If your baby is unconscious (she does not respond when call her name or tap the sole of her foot (do not shake her) but breathing, a modified version of the recovery position should be used until help arrives

If your baby is unconscious and not breathing, turn her on to her back, supporting her all along the length of her body as you do so. Perform rescue breathing and, if necessary, CPR (see page 95).

Call for help and get another adult to contact the emergency services (911). If you are alone, begin resuscitating your baby but after one minute, ring the emergency services yourself, while maintaining rescue breathing.

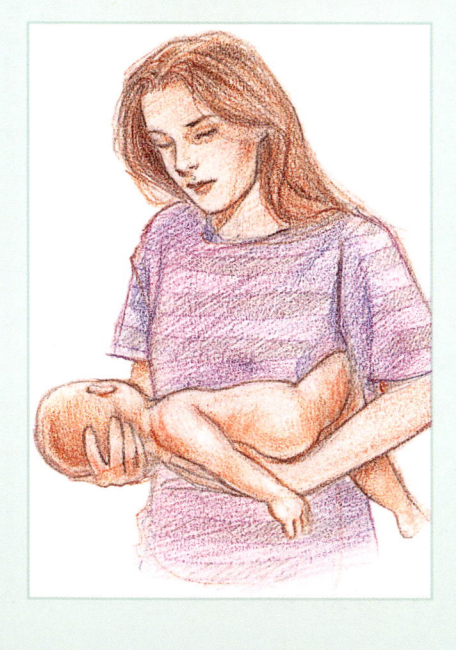

Recovery position
Cradle your baby in your arms with her head tilted slightly downward. This keeps her airway open by preventing her tongue from rolling back into her throat and allows any liquid, including vomit, to drain from her mouth.

RESCUE BREATHING

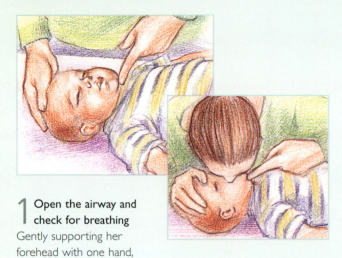

1 Open the airway and check for breathing
Gently supporting her forehead with one hand, place a finger (not the thumb) of your other hand under her jaw. Tilt her head back by lifting the chin gently. See if you can detect any movement in the chest or feel any breath against your cheek.

2 Give two to five slow breaths
If there is no breathing, open your mouth wide and take a breath in, filling your cheeks with air. Cover your baby's nose and mouth with your mouth and slowly breathe out for 1–2 seconds. Look to make sure her chest rises when you breathe into her; stop breathing into her once it has risen and let her chest fall when you stop. Repeat until you have given two effective breaths.

3 Look for signs of circulation
To see if your baby's heart is beating, look, listen and feel for breathing, coughing, movement or any other signs of life. If breathing starts, hold her in the recovery position (page 94). If her chest doesn't rise and there is no breath, begin Cardiopulmonary Resuscitation (CPR).

If your baby vomits
Quickly turn her head and body to the side; wipe away any vomit to ensure it doesn't get into her lungs. Continue rescue breathing.

CPR (CARDIOPULMONARY RESUSCITATION)

1 Locate the compression point
Place your baby flat on her back on a firm surface (you don't have to remove her clothing). Hold her forehead with one hand and position the index finger of your other hand just under the midpoint of an imaginary line running between her nipples. Place the next two fingers underneath. Raise your index finger. You should be at the bottom of the breastbone.

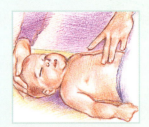

2 Compress the chest 30 times
Using your two fingers and bending your elbow, push down one-third to half the depth of his chest, then release. Use a steady down and up pace. Give five compressions in 3 seconds (100 every minute).

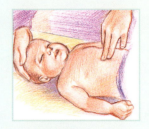

3 Give two rescue breaths
After 30 compressions, check your baby's mouth and give two rescue breaths lasting 1–2 seconds. Repeat the 30 compressions. Alternate two breaths and 30 compressions, checking the mouth after every set until help arrives. If your baby's color improves or there are signs of circulation, stop the compressions but continue rescue breathing until your baby starts breathing or help arrives.

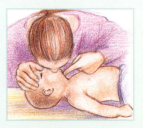

INDEX